The Story of Vic & Sade

❖ ❖ ❖ ❖

BY BILL IDELSON

THE STORY OF VIC & SADE
© 2007 Bill Idelson

All rights reserved.

No part of this book may be reproduced in any form or by any means, electronic, mechanical, digital, photocopying or recording, except for the inclusion in a review, without permission in writing from the the publisher.

PUBLISHED IN THE USA BY:

BearManor Media
PO Box 71426
Albany, GA 31708
www.BearManorMedia.com

LIBRARY OF CONGRESS CATALOGING-IN-PUBLICATION DATA:

Idelson, Billy.
  The story of Vic & Sade / by Bill Idelson.
    p. cm.
  ISBN-13: 978-1-59393-061-5
  1. Vic and Sade (Radio program)   I. Title.
PN1991.77.V5I34 2006
791.44'72--dc22

   2006027962

Printed in the United States.

Cover Design and Layout by Howie Idelson.

Interior Design and Layout by Valerie Thompson.

Table of Contents

Foreword —————————————————— 1

Acknowledgments ——————————————— 4

The Story of Vic & Sade ——————————— 5

Chapter Two ————————————————— 24

Chapter Three ———————————————— 44

Chapter Four ————————————————— 68

Chapter Five ————————————————— 99

Chapter Six—1933 —————————————— 119

Chapter Seven—1934 ————————————— 143

Chapter Eight—1935 ————————————— 184

Chapter Nine—1936 —————————————— 235

Last Chapter ————————————————— 291

Dedicated to Seemah,
for her patience

Foreword

Of the many societies that abound in the fastnesses of Los Angeles, the *Vic and Sadists* is perhaps the strangest. It has no charter, no permanent address, no officers, no constitution, no regular meetings, and only six members—Ray Bradbury, Stan Freberg, Bill Idelson, Martin Halperin, Robert Ahmanson, and myself. The first two and the last are essentially writers; Idelson is an actor; Halperin, a technical wizard and collector of Old-Time Radio memorabilia; Ahmanson, a philanthropist, head of the Ahmanson Foundation and longtime supporter of OTR. They have in common a major fixation—devotion to the memory of a daytime radio program named *Vic and Sade*, a landmark comedy serial which began in the summer of 1932 on the Blue Network of NBC and continued off and on, including a television incarnation, into 1957.

At a typical Vic and Sadist meeting, archival V&S programs are played, to the re-amazement of the members that so great a family comedy survived for so long by maintaining superb quality.

The idol of the *Sadist* group is Idelson, who at the beginning of his career as a member of the Gook household was drafted, against his will, to play the role of Rush, the adopted son of Vic and Sade. Bill at first hated working in radio, an attitude not likely to have been appreciated by fellow performers and management, and it took a bit of seasoning before he came around to like his role. But the quality of the writing, directing and acting that Idelson encountered in the studio quickly won him over.

One day, long after *Vic and Sade* ended its run and creator, Paul Rhymer, had died, I read in the *Los Angeles Times* a letter to the editor written by the same Bill Idelson. It had such clarity, cogency and force that I realized Bill's writing was as exceptional as his acting, and I phoned to tell him so. Maybe this small homage persuaded him, many years later, to invite me to write the foreword to the volume that you now hold in your hands.

What Idelson does in these pages is to explore the mountain of *Vic and Sade* scripts preserved in a Wisconsin archive, to trace the characters and devices that Rhymer used in developing story lines, characters and relationships, and altogether to illuminate the whole from within.

There have been many other accounts and tributes, long and short, one of the best a six-page entry in John Dunning's remarkable *Encyclopedia of Old-Time Radio*. Just reading the names of characters, institutions and products familiar to the Gook family—among them Steve Chestbutter, Robert and Slobert Hink, Rishigan Fishigan of Shishigan, Michigan, Ike Kneesuffer, Pom Pom Cordova, Four Fisted Frank Futterman, Charles Razorscum, Chuck and Dottie Brainfeeble, The Drowsy Venus Chapter of the Sacred Stars of the Milky Way, The Tiny Petite Pheasant Feather Tea Shoppe, The Institute for the Incurably Shy, The Ohio State Home for the Freckled, chocolate-flavored sandpaper, beef punkles, limberschwartz cheese—all give readers a good time.

One comes away from reading Idelson's panography with the conviction that Paul Rhymer ranks in the top echelon of American humorists along with Ring Lardner ("'Shut up,' he explained"); Mark Twain ("Wagner's music is better than it sounds") and Finley Dunne ("No matter whether the constitution follows the flag or not, the Supreme Court follows the election returns.").

Not until late in the book does Idelson get down to the character of Rhymer, an outlook which in some ways is a surprise. Many of the qualities inferred earlier from the qualities of the family in "the small house halfway up in the next block" are either muted or transformed. There is a raunchiness to his humor, expressed through coarse sexual allusions such as "twat" and "snatch." But nothing dims in Idelson's reading of the man and his work. There is a poignancy in their late-in-life encounters. Their last meeting provides a touching end to a brisk and prolific working relationship:

"When I left to drive back to the airport in my rented Ford coupe, I looked up in the rear-view mirror and saw him standing on the street corner, keeping me in sight as long as he could, a white-haired, dignified man in a dark topcoat and dark felt hat, and I had a strong, almost overwhelming feeling that this was the last time I'd see him."

NORMAN CORWIN

Acknowledgments

A great debt of gratitude goes to those who helped make this book possible: Seemah, my wife; Barbara Schwarz, official librarian for *Vic and Sade*; Ben Ohmart and Valerie Thompson for their understanding; Howie Idelson for his artwork on *Gibby* and this cover; and the great Norman Corwin for his terrific introduction.

BILL IDELSON
SEPTEMBER 2006

The Story of Vic & Sade

Paul Rhymer, creator of "Vic and Sade," called by a prominent critic of the time, "The only genius to come out of radio," was driving a cab in Chicago when he was hired by NBC as a writer. They hired him on the strength of a short story he'd written for a national magazine. The story was about a guy who worked in a factory and, while operating some machinery, cut off his thumb. The other guys at work were curious about how he'd suffered his injury and, being an agreeable fellow, he offered to show them. In so doing, he cut off his other thumb.

Paul worked in the writers' room with half a dozen other scribes, producing lead-ins for musical numbers and jokes for the Saturday night variety show. Clarence Menser, head of NBC radio in Chicago, suggested that he try his hand at a family show for daytime programming.

Paul's version of a family show was a story of a childless couple somewhat past the age of "Mad about You." It was called "Vic & Sade." NBC showed its luke-warm confidence by scheduling the program at 8:30 A.M., when viewer attention was practically nil. And the first ten days or so indicated that the wise guys at the network were probably right. Paul went for jokes.

SADE: Remember, Vic, when you said every time I sat on your lap like this it almost broke your heart?

VIC: Uh-huh. And now it breaks my cigars. Listen, baby....

They were in trouble. As Sade says in script number four:

SADE: ....and it frightens me to think there's nothing for us to talk about.

Menser suggested they bring in another character, a child, but, since they'd started off without children, it posed something of a problem. In script number seven, Vic and Sade are sitting on the porch and the conversation is desultory. Some gossip, noticing people passing on the street with a low-toned comment after they've passed, some talk about buying a car and then Sade indicates there's something on her mind. After some pressure from Vic she comes out with it:

SADE: I want to adopt a child.

VIC: Adopt—a—child!

SADE: Yes, Vic.

(Little Pause)

VIC: No!

SADE: Vic, I . . . .

VIC: No!

(Little Pause)

SADE: Vic, I . . . .

VIC: No!

(Little Pause)

SADE: *(In A Wee Small Voice)* Vic, isn't this Mr. and Mrs. Hess coming down the street?

VIC: Dunno.

SADE: It's Mr. and Mrs. Hess

VIC: *(Nothing)*

SADE: .... AND THEIR LITTLE BOY Harold.

VIC: *(Nothing)*

SADE: They're going down to the square and back, I guess. Get some ice cream.

VIC: *(Nothing)*

SADE: Hello, Mr. Hess, hello, Mrs. Hess. Hello, Harold.

VIC: (*Sourly*) That's the kid that walked on our radishes, isn't it?

SADE: Yes, Aren't you . . . aren't you going to say hello, Vic?

VIC: No.

SADE: Mr. and Mrs. Hess are waving. Go on, Vic, wave.

VIC: (*With Very Ill Grace*) 'Lo, Mr. Hess. 'Lo, Mis' Hess.

SADE: Vic.

(Little Pause)

SADE: Vic.

VIC: Yeah.

SADE: Vic, I . . . .

VIC: No!

SADE: Vic, put your arm around me again. Please.

VIC: Uh. (*Surrenders His Arm Under Pressure*)

SADE: That's it. Vic, please listen, I . . . .

VIC: No!

(*Little Pause*)

VIC: The idea is preposterous. Adopting a baby!

SADE: I didn't say a baby, Vic.

VIC: What'd you say?

SADE: I said a child.

VIC: Same thing. I can see myself trampling around the house in the middle of the night, walking the floor. My home in an uproar all the time. My wife raising Cain. One expense after the other. Misery, sickness, trouble . . .

SADE: Oh, no, Vic. We could get a little girl. One about three—or four—or five. She'd be so sweet and we'd love her so.

VIC: No! I'm going inside. Comin'?

SADE: Please stay out here a little while longer, Vic.

VIC: Uh.

SADE: Please.

(*Little Pause*)

VIC: 'Lo, Pete. (*Calling*)

SADE: Hello, Mr. Donahue. (*And To Vic*) He looks better than he's looked in a long time, don't you think, Vic?

VIC: (*Aff.*) Uh.

(*Little Pause*)

VIC: Ain't I company enough for ya, Sade?

SADE: Oh, Vic, you know you are. You're everything! . . . Vic, you're so much to me . . . so very, very, very much . . . that I . . . that I have to have somebody else to taper off on.

VIC: (*A Trifle Irritably*) Now, what on earth do you mean by that?

SADE: I mean that I love you so much that I . . . I just choke up inside. I'm so crammed full of love for you that I need . . . I need someone else to . . . to help me love you. And a little girl . . .

VIC: No!

SADE: A little girl to do for and make over . . .

VIC: No!

SADE: Vic, there'd be three of us. And each of us would have two to love. As it is, Vic, you and I just love each other so much . . . and all we've got is that, and it leaves us kind of inarticulate and cramped sort of.

VIC: Don't know what you're talking about.

SADE: Listen, Vic. We need something to share . . . something to be interested in . . . something to work for. And a little girl . . .

VIC: Little girl, nothin'. Little boy.

SADE: Oh, Vic . . .

VIC: What?

SADE: A little boy.

VIC: (*Irritably*) What about a little boy?

SADE: You said . . .

VIC: I didn't say anything of the sort.

(Little Pause)

SADE: Just think, Vic. A little boy . . . and his name could be 'Vic' . . . Vic Gook. We could get a real husky little boy. A smart little boy like you were . . .

VIC: Now listen, Sade, don't try to soft-soap the old man. I'm going inside.

SADE: Vic, wait . . .

VIC: Nope. I gotta go inside.

SADE: What for?

VIC: Gotta get a cigar.

SADE: I'll go in and get it.

VIC: Don't bother.

SADE: I'll go in and get your cigar. Now don't you move.

VIC: Uh. (*We Hear Sade Get Up And Go, And Then There's A Little Pause. Finally Vic Begins To Chuckle To Himself. Chuckles A Little Louder. And A Little Louder*)

VIC: (*To Himself, Chuckling*) Vic. Vic Rodney Gook. (*Chuckles, And Some More*) Now, listen, Buster, don't try to pull the wool over your old man's eyes. Know what I done when I was a kid and got licked in a fight? I took some boxing lessons from a big kid in our block, see, and I hit a punching bag for two hours every night after school, and finally I rounded up the chap that licked me, see . . . rounded him up right on the school-yard, and if I didn't whale the daylights outa that bully . . . (*Chuckles*) . . . why, Vic, when he got home his maw didn't know him. Yessir, I . . .

SADE: Vic, what are you saying?

VIC: Nothin'.

SADE: You were talking. I heard you.

VIC: Gimme that cigar.

SADE: What were you saying, Vic?

VIC: This darned old cigar . . . feels kinda dry. Gosh, I . . .

SADE: Vic, I heard what you said. (*Joyously*) Oh, Vic . . .

VIC: Hey, ain't this Jeff Swanson coming down the street?

SADE: (*Joyously*) Uh-huh . . . (*Calling Brightly*) Hello, Mr. Swanson.

VIC: 'Lo, Mr. Swanson. (*Aside*) Aw, Sade. (*And A Good Throaty Chuckle*)

From the moment they even begin talking about the child, the show changes character. In show number eight, Mother is still there, but she's good for a couple of jokes and that's all.

SADE: Vic.

VIC: What?

SADE: 'Member what we were talking about last night?

VIC: No.

SADE: About . . . adopting a child.

VIC: No.

SADE: Yes, you do. Vic . . .

VIC: Sade, that's out—definitely out.

SADE: Vic . . .

VIC: Sade, I tell you that's out. We adopt no child. We adopt no child! Do you hear?

SADE: Yes, Vic.

(*Little Pause*)

VIC: Sade, I know how you feel about this adopting a child business. And I appreciate it, too.

SADE: Are you sure you do?

VIC: Positively. Oh, I've thought about it. Quite a lot. But it's no go.

SADE: All right, Vic.

VIC: You're not . . . hurt?

SADE: No.

VIC: Don't feel bad?

SADE: No.

❖ ❖ ❖ ❖

Sade asks Vic to teach her how to play solitaire, and he begins. She is dense about the game; while he perseveres, she mentions casually that she wrote to Mary Meadows, a girl she went to school with. Vic pays small attention, as she tells that Mary's husband is in the wholesale grocery business and has made no money in the last year and a half. These are Depression years, of course, and Vic observes that many folks are in the same boat.

SADE: . . . Did I tell ya, Vic, Mary's got four children.

VIC: (*Neg.*) Uh-huh. That red five'll play up there, Sade. That's it.

SADE: I think Mary and her family are in awful bad shape. Don't even get enough to eat, I guess. They got two little girls and two little boys. Awful cute kids, Mary says. The oldest boy's nine, and the youngest . . . a little girl, Hannah . . . is two and a half. Mary says . . .

VIC: Sade, are you going to play cards or are you going to talk? You went and put a red card on another red card.

SADE: Oh, did I? Here—that fixes it, doesn't it? Gee, this is lotsa fun.

VIC: Yeah—great game, solitaire.

SADE: Mary said in her letter—she didn't actually come out and say so . . . but she hinted that if we wanted to, we could take one of her children for a little while until . . .

VIC: (*Waking Up*) What?

SADE: . . . just for a little while. Until her husband gets on his feet again. It would be kind of nice if we did, I thought. A child wouldn't be much in the way. Be kinda company for me through the day.

VIC: Sade, what are you trying to come over on me?

SADE: Nothing, Vic, nothing.

VIC: All right, then. Now look!—you've gone and put another red card . . .

SADE: Oh, I see, Vic. Just forgot for a moment.

(Card Playing Interlude)

VIC: Which one of her kids does this friend of yours want to shove off on us?

SADE: She doesn't want to shove any of 'em off on us, Vic. She just thought we'd like to have Vic come and stay with us a little while.

VIC: Vic?

SADE: Yes, that's the name of her oldest boy. He's nine. Mary never said so, Vic, but I think he was named for you.

VIC: 'Zat so?

SADE: Uh-huh. Real sweet of her, I think.

VIC: Well, we're not taking on any more mouths to feed. Sade, you've done it again . . . the black seven . . . the black seven.

SADE: Oh, yes. Uh-huh (*Giggles*)

VIC: Here—let me finish. Your mind's not on it.

(Card Playing Interlude)

VIC: What kind of a boy is this boy Vic?

SADE: Real sweet, I guess. Looks something like you, Mary says.

VIC: How's she know how I look?

SADE: She's got lot of pictures of you I sent her.

VIC: Oh.

SADE: He weighs five pounds more than he really should for his age, he's so sturdy. And he's a grade ahead in school.

VIC: (*Non-Committal*) Uh.

SADE: Of course we couldn't take him, though. He's kind of a rough-neck.

VIC: Rough-neck?

SADE: Yes. Mary says he's pitcher on his school team . . . and he's got the house cluttered up with bats and balls and things. And he refuses to be anything when he grows up but pitcher for the New York Giants.

VIC: Huh. How long would we have to keep this kid if he came?

SADE: Oh, I don't think we want him, Vic. After thinking about it a minute I can see you're perfectly right. He'd be an awful nuisance . . . and an awful expense too. Besides—one Victor Gook in the house is enough.

VIC: Sure. The idea of a nine-year old pitcher living with us is preposterous.

SADE: Sure.

(*Little Pause*)

VIC: Still, though, since this Mary was such a friend of yours . . . I mean . . . a person really owes his fellow man . . . That is . . .

SADE: Vic, doesn't the red six go on the black seven?

VIC: (**Flustered**) Uh . . . Yeah . . . Sure. Sure. On the black seven. As I was sayin' though, Sade, after all, a few weeks wouldn't hurt any . . . or a few months.

SADE: Vic, that card goes up, doesn't it? Not down there . . .

VIC: Oh, sure . . . What's getting into me? Say, Sade, why don't you kinda drop a line to your friend and sorta tell her, you know, tell her . . .

SADE: Vic . . .

VIC: Yeah . . .

SADE: I already have. He's coming next week.

VIC: Who is?

SADE: Vic. Victor. The little baseball player.

VIC: *(Hard Boiled)* Now, listen here, Sade Gook, I . . .

SADE: (*Laughing Joyfully*) Vic! You've put the wrong card here . . . and here . . . and here . . . and here . . . and here . . .

(AS WE FADE OUT)

My father ran a speakeasy all during Prohibition, so I guess he was a criminal, although I didn't think of him that way. And I guess I was a criminal, too, because I spent a lot of time in that saloon and actually helped Dad make the booze down in our basement. There was a locked room down there where Pop kept his alcohol and stuff which he got from the Al Capone gang in Cicero.

Two of his regular customers, along with the policemen, firemen and mayor of Forest Park, Illinois (our town), were Art Van Harvey and his wife. Art had spent most of his working life selling ads for the **Hog Breeders Journal**, but his real goal was to become an actor. Now that he was retired, he spent most of his time in the lobby of NBC, nineteenth floor of the Merchandise Mart, hoping to land a job in radio. Wonder of wonders, he won the audition and got the job of Vic in the new radio show, "Vic and Sade." Since the new show had so little hope of becoming anything, the brass apparently didn't mind using an absolute neophyte who had never had a single job in show business.

Art and my Dad were close and, whenever they were in Bennie's Bar, Art confided all his adventures in the acting business to my Father. Now he told Dad that they were thinking of adding a character to his show, and it was to be a young boy. "Hell," said my Dad, "my son Billy is a radio actor!" And it was true. I had played the part of "Skeezix" and a small part in another show on WGN.

The negative side of this little coincidence was that I hated acting! And I had announced this to my Mother. But when the call came she accepted it; after all, this was the Depression and no one refused work. But I hit the ceiling. I wouldn't go! She calmed me down—it was to be for only four days. I gave in. But it was only for four days. Remember!

Bernardine Flynn was from Madison, Wisonsin where her Father owned a clothing store. Bern had ambitions for the stage and took a flyer at Broadway. But in spite of her beauty she got only small roles and decided to try radio in Chicago, where it was rumored there was lots going on. She wired her friend, Don Ameche, who had remained in New York: "Come out here. There's work!"

Script nine opens with Vic all alone in the living room practicing a speech.

VIC: (*With Oratorical Splendor*) Gentlemen of the bookkeeping department of the Consolidated Kitchenware Company: I can't tell you how honored it makes me feel to be asked to be privileged to address you at this time. As I look into the faces of all you old friends and co-workers, I am reminded of a litter of hogs that belonged to a certain farmer . . .

Sade arrives and Vic makes her listen to the speech. There is a call from Mis' Fisher, the old lady who lives alone next door, to ask if Vic is all right. She can hear him yelling and has seen him through the window waving his arms around wildly. Sade explains he's O.K. then Vic tells Sade why he's especially concerned about the speech:

VIC: . . . If the boys ask me to talk I wanta make a good showing. Old Ruebush'll be there and everybody. Your old man's kinda got to make good now, Sade . . . (*Chuckles*) . . . ya know?

SADE: What do you mean, Vic?

VIC: Takin' on another mouth to feed and all.

SADE: (*Laughs*) That's right. Gee, won't it be wonderful?

VIC: I don't know. Might be all right; then again it might not. When's the boy coming?

SADE: I don't know for sure. Some day next week. I'm having so much fun getting ready for him. Yesterday I . . .

VIC: Aw, Sade, pipe down. I got to write this speech.

VIC: (*More Or Less To Himself*) Kitchenware may be likened unto a white dove of peace that spreads his wings over . . .

The doorbell rings and it's the man from Croucher's store bringing a little trunk. Sade bought it for the boy to keep his clothes in. It costs twelve dollars and Vic hits the ceiling. Already the kid is costing them a fortune. In the midst of his tirade the doorbell rings again and a small bicycle is delivered. Sade wants to know where that came from.

VIC: It was a real bargain . . . only thirty-four dollars and a quarter . . . I . . .

Sade can't be angry. In fact, she thinks Vic is an old darling. Vic can't resist trying the bike out and rides it around the living room as the phone rings and Sade must explain the latest strange sight to Mrs. Fisher.

In script number ten Vic comes home delirious over the good possibility of getting the head bookkeeper's job at the plant, due to Frank Witson's transfer to Plant #5. But then the phone rings. It's the boss—Ruebush, wanting to know what Vic thinks of Charlie Kilgore. Vic is sick with the conviction it's Charlie who is getting the job. At the end of the script, Vic calls Charlie and tells him that whichever of them is selected . . . there's no hard feelings.

Number eleven. Vic is sick in bed with a cold, but it's obvious that low spirits and fear are involved. And Sade, for the first time, becomes the forceful, Midwestern, old-fashioned wife:

SADE: Now, Vic Gook, get this . . . when you're sick . . . or when anybody in my family's sick, I'm the boss. Understand?

Bern was perfect for this role. And Sade began to grow out of a combination of Paul's experience and the actor's personality. There was this tough, indomitable streak in Bern, and Paul seized on it and fitted it in with his picture of his own Mother.

Vic feels he's a failure, but Sade jokes and bullies him out of it. There is shouting outside supplied by everybody in the studio: "We want the new boss." Vic is stunned, then goes outside to make a speech. Vic is now Chief Accountant of the Bookkeeping Department of Consolidated Kitchenware Company, Plant #14, a job he keeps to the end.

In number twelve, Vic has the new job but confesses that his secretary has him intimidated. He's never dictated before and gets tongue-tied when he has to.

VIC: I have got kind of an important job now.

SADE: Oh, I know you have, Vic. I get thrilled right down to my toes every time I think of it. Everything's so wonderful. Everything.

VIC: (*Chuckles*) I . . . I wonder if the kid . . . when he comes . . . wonder if he'll think I . . . I'm . . . I . . .

SADE: Sure he will. He'll think you're the biggest man in the world. I know he will.

VIC: What time tomorrow's he comin', Sade?

SADE: Sometime in the early evening. A man that's driving through in a car is going to drop him . . .

We have a picture of the times. His parents can't come—can't afford to. And certainly they have no car of their own. That was a luxury that even Vic and Sade never achieved.

The central plot of this script concerns several dogs delivered by well-meaning friends for the new boy who's coming. But it's also full of Vic's fears of how much man he is—now that he's faced with becoming a Father so abruptly. After all, even his secretary frightens him. He's full of a wild ambition to be something for the boy. There is a feeling in these scripts of something so right. The emotions are vital and accurate, even though Paul, at this time was not even married. But everything was falling into place. The characters were taking hold . . . there was a feeling of longevity. You wanted to know more about these people—to live with them. Maybe because there was so much affection between them—real love covered with funniness.

In script number thirteen, Vic and Sade are sitting on the porch waiting at nearly ten o'clock in the evening. They've been waiting for hours for the arrival of the boy. He was supposed to get there around seven-thirty, but, as Vic says, the trip is about four hundred miles and "ya can never tell about long automobile trips like that."

Sade's mind is in a turmoil of worry and doubt—perhaps Mary has changed her mind. Maybe it would be better if she had. If they have the boy and then have to give him up . . . and you hear things about adopted children . . . but it's all rationalization, she confesses finally. She's desperate to have the child and is only worried that something has happened to thwart this desire. Vic carries her, almost feverish, in to the living room and they sit on the couch. Her head is on his shoulder; she's determined to stay up until she knows whether he's coming or not . . .

VIC: Hey, I'll tell you what . . . (*Chuckles Foolishly*) . . . I'll tell you a story . . . one I sorta doped out to tell the kid.

SADE: All right, Vic.

VIC: Well, one time I was traveling in Madagascar, and I had a real sharp sword. A sword nine feet long. At that time I was ten feet tall myself with green whiskers.

SADE: (*Giggling Sleepily*)

VIC: Well sir, that sword of mine was the sharpest sword that ever was. It was so sharp that I could cut right through a tree and never hurt the tree, that sword was so sharp. Went through the tree just like electricity. (*Lowers His Voice*) Well, in Madagascar they got apple trees a mile high . . . and ya know what I done? I put some vanilla on my sword and run the sword through one of those apple trees. And I done it again. And again. D'you know, I climbed up to the top of that tree and picked on of those apples . . . and it was vanilla flavored. Yes, sir, vanilla flavored. And I ate nineteen bushel of those vanilla-flavored apples, and I got so darn fat I couldn't climb down that tree. It was a mile high, ya know. So I just shook that tree and shook it and shook it, and all the apples fell off and piled up . . . and I just slid down the pile. (*Softly*) Sade. Sade.. (*Chuckles*) . . . and then I went to Australia with those apples and sold 'em for ten cents apiece and made ten million dollars. They paid me off in nickels and I put all those nickels in my pocket, and I had a hole in my pocket and every single last one of those nickels fell in the river. (*Almost Asleep Himself*) So I took my sword and I . . . and I . . . I took my sword and I . . . (*Gentle Snore: Continued For A Few Seconds*)

(*Knock*)

(*A Little Louder Snore*)

(*A Little Louder Snore*)

LITTLE BOY: (*Timidly*) Hello.

(*Little Pause*)

LITTLE BOY: Hello.

(*Little Pause*)

LITTLE BOY: Hello, anybody home?

(*A Good Snouty Snore From Vic*)

LITTLE BOY: (*Laughing And Shaking The Snorer*) Hey, mister, wake up! Wake up! C'mon. (*. . . And To Theme*)

END OF SCRIPT

Chapter Two

I was the little boy. It wasn't my first job in radio. More than a year before I had played the part of "Skeezix" in WGN's "Gasoline Alley." After that, there were several other jobs and I hated it. It took time from play and my friends, and the work itself, with its tensions and frustrations, was terribly unpleasant for me. I made a screaming pronouncement to my family that never again would I do a radio show, and that was that. When my mother informed me she had accepted a job for me from NBC to appear on some show I'd never heard of, I went into a tantrum, crying and shouting and throwing myself onto the couch. She mollified me by saying that the job was for four days only. She was telling the truth.

The original offer was for four days . . . NBC wanted a chance to try me out as well as the character. If I wasn't satisfactory, they could have tried another boy, or, if the character did not work in some way, they could have gone to a different age boy, a girl, or abandoned the idea of another character altogether. They were leaving their options open.

The show went on the air at 8:30 A.M. We met an hour earlier for rehearsal, in the 19th floor lobby of NBC, in the Merchandise Mart. We read the script sitting on the black leather benches along the wall; Menser, who was directing the show himself at the time, sat across a space of green carpet at the receptionist's desk. There was no one else around at this hour. We couldn't rehearse in studio "B" where we broadcast, because Walter Blaufuss and his orchestra were in there playing the "Morning Serenade." So we rehearsed in the lobby and went into the studio a few moments before air time.

I probably showed up rather sullenly for that first show, although I don't remember exactly. But, as I recall, I liked Bernardine and Van pretty much at first sight. And Menser, dark and authoritative, inspired a bit of awe. He was stern but kindly, I felt, and he seemed to like me. There was also a subtle difference in atmosphere about this show from the ones I had done previously—a feeling of something special—but certainly nothing to change my opinion of radio acting.

At about 8:25 we pushed open the double set of heavy doors and entered studio "B," which was a large studio used mostly for musical programs. A blast of peppy early morning music came from the twenty-piece orchestra that occupied the center of the room. Walter Blaufuss was up in front, on a small platform, waving away uncritically with his baton, turning to nod and smile at us as we entered. In the far corner of the studio was a square beige cloth tent, open on one side, that dramatic shows used to avoid a boomy sound. Inside the tent were two microphones: one for Van and Bern, and a lower one for me.

We made our way toward this tent as Walter concluded his program. The announcer wrapped up "Morning Serenade," rang his chimes and then the orchestra broke into our theme, "Oh, You Beautiful Doll." A short introduction from the announcer and we were on the air.

The musicians were now laying aside their instruments as quietly as they could, but with an accidental squeak and bang here and there, and tip-toeing outside for a smoke. A few remained, sitting in their chairs, some holding their violins on their knees, to listen. If something struck them funny, they would laugh out loud. Toward the end of the show the musicians began filing back in again, taking their seats, ready to play our closing theme.

In that first show, of course, I had almost nothing to do. I said my lines and left the studio. One down and three to go!

Here is script number fourteen:

SADE: (*Softly*) Vic. Vic.

VIC: (*Sleepily*) Urp . . . awg . . . posh . . . ump . . . choo.

SADE: (*Softly*) Vic, wake, up.

VIC: Unk . . . lemme 'lone . . . get away . . .

SADE: (***Shakes Him***) Vic. Vic.

VIC: Raw . . . buh . . . hee . . . (***Awake***) Huh?

SADE: Vic, will ya . . . kinda . . . kinda . . . get up?

VIC: What ya mean "kinda" get up? What's the matter? Sick?

SADE: No, the little boy . . . Victor . . .

VIC: 'Smatter with 'im?

SADE: He's homesick, I guess. Been laying awake for the longest time. Sobbing to himself.

VIC: What time is it?

SADE: A little after five-thirty.

VIC: A little after five-thirty. Gosh, Sade, it's the middle of the night.

SADE: I know, Vic, but it just tears my heart to hear him. I've gone to the door of his room half a dozen times. He's never been away from home before . . . never slept in any bed but his own. C'mon, get up, Vic.

VIC: What can I do, Sade?

SADE: I dunno, Vic . . . thought we might entertain him some way. Make him forget he's homesick. Gee, he's such a little tiny boy and all. And so brave. He didn't let out a peep when I put him to bed. Just stood there with his little shirt off and waited for me to leave the room.

VIC: (*Chuckling*) Wouldn't take off his pants, huh?

SADE: (*Giggling A Little*) No . . . he took off his shoes and stockings and shirt, and then he just looked at me and waited. And when I went towards the door he said, "Good night" . . . very, very solemnly and respectfully—like the little gentleman he is. And then he stood and watched me. I went to the door and as I was going out I looked around and already the tears had started. He looked the other way so I wouldn't see. I went out and closed the door, and stood outside a moment . . . and then he broke loose. Cried as though his heart would break.

VIC: Tired from that long automobile trip prob'ly.

SADE: That had something to do with it, I suppose. Vic, c'mon and get up. We'll amuse him some way. These first few days are going to be awful hard on him. What do you say?

VIC: O.K., kiddo. Hey, let's sneak into his room wheeling that bicycle. That'll cheer him up, I'll bet my shirt. He hasn't got a bicycle, has he?

SADE: No . . . I asked him last night. He never had one, he said. But I gathered he'd like to have one.

VIC: (*Chuckling*) Let's go!

SADE: Wait, Vic. He wouldn't want us to know he's been crying. You go get the bicycle. I'll knock on his door.

VIC: (*On His Way*) Sure. Golly, don't know when I've

been up this early before . . . ain't hardly daylight yet. I . . . (*Fade*)

SADE: (*Knocks Softly*) Victor.

(*Little Pause*)

VICTOR: (*Inside*) Yes'm.

SADE: Good morning, Victor.

VICTOR: Good morning.

(*Little Pause*)

SADE: Did you sleep well, Victor?

VICTOR: Yes, ma'm. Thank you.

(*Little Pause*)

SADE: Was the . . . was the bed comfortable?

VICTOR: Yes, ma'm. Thank you.

SADE: (*Little Pause*) You . . . you didn't wear your pajamas.

VICTOR: No,'m. I slept in my under-pants.

SADE: (*Not Knowing What To Say*) Oh.

(*Little Pause*)

SADE: I . . . I suppose your mother kisses you in the morning, Victor?

VICTOR: Yes'm.

SADE: A... may I kiss you, Victor?

VICTOR: No, ma'm.

SADE: Uh-huh.

VICTOR: I don't like kissin'.

SADE: Uh-huh.

(*Little Pause*)

SADE: Would you like to get up?

VICTOR: Yes, ma'm.

SADE: You needn't call me "ma'm," Victor.

VICTOR: What shall I call you?

SADE: I... I don't know. (*Little Pause*) I guess... guess you can call me "ma'm."

VICTOR: Yes, ma'm.

SADE: Want me to help you dress?

VICTOR: No, ma'm.

SADE: Uh-huh.

(*Little Pause*)

SADE: Is that a scar on your arm, Victor?

VICTOR: Yeah... got hit with a stick that had a nail in it.

SADE: Uh-huh.

VICTOR: Got one on this arm too. Vaccination.

SADE: Uh-huh.

VICTOR: You got a vaccination scar?

SADE: Yes.

VICTOR: Lemme see it.

SADE: See.

VICTOR: It's bigger'n mine. Red Williams's got a bigger one than yours even.

SADE: Has he?

VICTOR: Yeah . . . he made his bigger with a piece of glass. (*Laughs And Is Joined By Sade*) He got a lickin' for it.

SADE: Did he?

VICTOR: (*Polite Again*) Yes, ma'm.

(*Little Pause*)

SADE: Want me to help you with your tie?

VICTOR: No, ma'm.

(*Little Pause*)

SADE: You're short a tooth in front, aren't you?

VICTOR: Uh-huh . . . pulled it out myself.

SADE: Gee, I'll bet it hurt.

VICTOR: Yeah . . . a little bit. Got 'nother one coming in though. See?

SADE: Uh-huh.

VICTOR: Got a tooth gone in the back too. Back here. (*Talks A Little With His Finger In His Mouth, Unintelligibly, Of Course, They Both Laugh*)

VIC: (*Coming In*) Good morning, young fella.

VICTOR: Good morning, sir.

VIC: How'd ya sleep?

VICTOR: Fine, thank you, sir.

VIC: That's good. Gosh, I'm all out of breath, Sade. Just ran around the block forty times.

SADE: Did you, Vic?

VIC: Yeah. D'you ever run around the block forty times, Vic?

VICTOR: No, sir.

VIC: I hadda run around the block this morning. Y'see. I got a watch that doesn't go very good . . . so I hadda run around the block forty times or it'd stop.

VICTOR: (*Laughing*) Aw, you're foolin'. (*All Three Laugh Heartily*)

SADE: I'll run down and get us something to eat. Are you hungry, Victor?

VICTOR: Yes, ma'm. A . . . don't go to no trouble.

SADE: Why, you darling. Listen, I'm going down and make some wheat cakes. Like wheat cakes?

VICTOR: Pancakes?

SADE: Yes. Pancakes.

VICTOR: Yes, I like 'em.

VIC: Wait a minute, Sade. I was just trying out that bicycle I bought and it don't fit me.

SADE: Don't fit you?

VIC: No, it's too small. Don't know what on earth I'm gonna do with it. The man won't take it back now that I've used it. Wonder if I could sell it to anybody.

SADE: Maybe Mis' Fisher'd like to buy it.

VIC: I don't know. (*Going Out The Door*) Wait a minute. I'll show it to you.

SADE: Gee, that's too bad. Bought a bicycle and it's too small.

VICTOR: Yes, ma'm.

VIC: (*Coming In*) It's a dandy bicycle too . . . coaster brake . . . siren horn . . . tool kit . . . saddle seat . . .

VICTOR: (*Gasps Involuntarily*) Jimminy! It's a peach.

VIC: Don't know where I could sell it, do you, Vic?

VICTOR: How . . . how much is it?

VIC: Five cents. I paid more for it, but I've used it already so I guess I can't get such a fancy price. A nickel takes it.

VICTOR: I'll buy it. I got a nickel.

VIC: Where's the nickel? I'm not handing out anything on credit.

VICTOR: (*Eagerly*) Here, sir.

VIC: Wait a minute till I bite it. I'm not selling this bicycle for no phony nickel.

VICTOR: Is . . . is it all right?

VIC: Yep . . . it's your bicycle.

VICTOR: Golly!

SADE: I'll run down and stir up the cakes. Call you when they're ready. (*She's Gone*)

VIC: All right, Sade. I'll show this fella how the bicycle works.

VICTOR: I know how it works, sir.

VIC: Aw get out. Now look here, Vic, see these pedals?

VICTOR: Yes, sir.

VIC: They're to put your feet on.

VICTOR: (*Laughing*) I know that.

VIC: Just want to make sure is all. See these handle-bars?

VICTOR: (*Laughing*) Yes, sir.

VIC: Ya put your hands on 'em . . . to guide with.

VICTOR: (*Laughing*) Uh-huh.

VIC: And this seat is to sit on.

VICTOR: Uh-huh.

VIC: Now, don't get mixed up, will ya? Don't go putting your feet on the seat and your hands on the pedals.

VICTOR: (*Laughing*) No, sir. Freck Johnson can ride without any hands.

VIC: Get out!

VICTOR: (*Laughing*) Yes, he can. And with his eyes shut too.

VIC: Impossible!

VICTOR: I saw him.

VIC: Bet he peeked.

VICTOR: No, sir. He was riding downtown that way once and he ran right into Mr. Peckinpaugh and tore his pants.

VIC: Whose pants?

VICTOR: Mr. Peckinpaugh's pants.

VIC: Mr. Peckinpaugh was riding the bicycle.

VICTOR: No, Freck Johnson was riding the bicycle.

VIC: . . . and tore his pants.

VICTOR: No, he tore Mr. Peckinpaugh's pants.

VIC: That's what I said. You were riding downtown with your eyes shut . . .

VICTOR: (*Laughing*) No, Freck Johnson was riding downtown, and . . .

VIC: I get ya, Steve.

VICTOR: Yes, sir.

VIC: Say, it's a funny thing, Vic. My name's the same as yours.

VICTOR: Uh-huh.

VIC: Well, nobody's coming in here named Vic. I had the name first and I'm gonna keep it. Understand?

VICTOR: (*Laughing*) Yes, sir.

VIC: Is there anything else you'd like to be called—besides Vic?

VICTOR: (*Eagerly*) Yes, call me "Rush."

VIC: Rush?

VICTOR: Yes, that's my middle name. I like it.

VIC: Ya don't like "Vic," huh? (*Belligerently*)

VICTOR: Yes, but I like Rush better.

VIC:	O.K., Rush. Say, Rush, what do you call . . . the . . . the lady?
VICTOR:	The nice lady . . . downstairs?
VIC:	Yes, what do you call her?
VICTOR:	I call her "ma'm."
VIC:	"Ma'm," huh? Listen, Rush . . . will ya do something for me?
VICTOR:	(*Eagerly*) Oh, yes, sir.
VIC:	Instead of calling her "ma'm," will ya call her "mom"?
VICTOR:	Mom?
VIC:	Yeah. The reason for that is one time I heard about a fella called all the ladies "mam" . . . and he strained a tonsil, and he couldn't never say anything else but "Pass the butter."
VICTOR:	(*Aghast*) You're foolin'.
VIC:	Fact. And I wouldn't want that to happen to you. So remember and call her "mom." Will you?
VICTOR:	Sure. Couldn't that man that strained his tonsils say anything but "Pass the butter"?
VIC:	Not a darn thing . . . that fella never got to first base.
VICTOR:	(*Slyly*) Bet he had a lotta butter, though. (*They Laugh*)

VIC:		Say, Rush, what ya gonna call me?
VICTOR:		I . . . I don't know, sir.
VIC:		Why don't you call me "gov" . . . short for governor, ya know.
VICTOR:		O.K. (*Little Pause*) I saw a governor once.
VIC:		Where'd you ever see a governor?
VICTOR:		At the zoo.
VIC:		At the zoo?
VICTOR:		Yeah . . . real big fella with fur all over . . .
VIC:		(*Laughing*) You mean you saw a gorilla. (*They Laugh*)
SADE:		(*Calling*) C'mon, Vic. C'mon, Victor. Breakfast.
VIC:		(*Whispering*) Don't forget about the "mom," kiddo.
VICTOR:		Mom.
VIC:		That's it. C'mon. Get on my back. I'm a bucking bronco by trade.
VICTOR:		Y'can't buck me off! (*And They Go Down Yelling*)
SADE:		Vic, you sit here. Victor, you sit here by me.
VIC:		This man's name is Rush, Sade. My name is Vic.
SADE:		Rush? Oh, I know. That was your mother's name before she was married . . . Rush.

VICTOR: Yes.

VIC: Sade, Rush and I were just talking about Mr. Peckinpaugh.

SADE: Were you? Here, Vic . . . Rush, take some syrup . . . lots of it.

VIC: Yeah . . . seems like Mr. Peckinpaugh was riding down the street backwards, and . . .

VICTOR: No, it was Freck Johnson, gov.

VIC: Oh, yeah, Freck Johnson, he . . .

SADE: What did Vic-Rush call you?

VIC: Calls me "gov" . . . short for governor.

SADE: Oh. (*Delighted*)

VIC: Well, Freck Johnson was riding down the street backwards . . .

VICTOR: (*Laughing*) Without any hands.

VIC: Without any hands. And he ran right square into Rush here who was standing with his eyes shut . . .

VICTOR: No, he ran into Mr. Peckinpaugh.

VIC: Well, if you know so much about it, you tell the story.

VICTOR: All right. Freck Johnson was riding the bicycle, Mom, and . . .

SADE: What'd you call me, dear?

VICTOR: Called you "mom."

SADE: Oh, did you. (*Delighted*) Go on . . . about Mr. Peckinpaugh.

VICTOR: Well, Freck Johnson run right into Mr. Peckinpaugh and tore his pants. Mr. Peckinpaugh was mad. (*They All Laugh*) He's funny, Mr. Peckinpaugh is. One time my little sister, Hannah . . . (*And The Very Word Brings Back His Homesickness*)

SADE: Yes, your little sister, Hannah . . .

(*Little Pause*)

VICTOR: May I be excused? I forgot something . . . upstairs.

SADE: Surely, Rush. Run along.

VIC: Go ahead, son.

(*He Goes Already Sobbing A Little Maybe*)

SADE: Oh, Vic, he's so homesick.

VIC: Yeah. Great kid, though.

SADE: Oh, isn't he!

VIC: Sade, think we oughta go up and kinda cheer him up?

SADE: No, let's leave him alone for a little while. Crying is such a relief for children and women.

VIC: I s'pose. Gee, he's a great kid. Calls me "gov." (*Chuckles*)

(*Little Pause*)

SADE: Vic . . .

VIC: Yeah, kiddo.

SADE: (*Swallows*) Vic, I think we better send him home . . . soon's we can.

VIC: Aw, he'll get over this homesickness, Sade.

SADE: It isn't that, Vic. It's that when he does go home, we'll be so homesick for him. Why, already, it'd . . . it'd pretty near kill me to part with him. Mary said in her letter we could keep him as long as we like . . . that's apt to mean months . . . or years.

VIC: Uh-huh.

SADE: . . . and there's no sense in our getting so wrapped up in him we couldn't let him go. Vic, what'll we do? Send him home?

VIC: Let's wait a while, anyway, Sade. Things like this always work out all right.

SADE: Do they?

VIC: Sure. They work themselves out. Look at the boy upstairs. He thinks he's got all the troubles there are in the world . . . being away from his mother and his little sister. Why, heck, in a day or so he'll be so full of ginger there'll be no holding him. That's the way it is with a lot of worrying people do. Things come out all right, Sade.

SADE: You've cheered me up, Vic.

VIC:	Sure I have . . . little ray of sunshine, that's your old man. Hey, how'd it be if I didn't go to work today? Just kinda stick around and keep the boy interested?
SADE:	That'd be lovely, Vic.
VIC:	All right. Listen: I'll go to the foot of the stairs and call the boy. Take him swimmin' over t' the lake. You come along.
SADE:	All right.
VIC:	(*Calling*) Rush! Rush!
VICTOR:	(*At A Little Distance*) Yes, gov.
VIC:	Wanta go swimmin'? Mom and me are goin'.
VICTOR:	I don' know, I . . .
VIC:	C'mon.
VICTOR:	Guess I better not.
VIC:	You're afraid. Afraid I'll duck ya.
VICTOR:	No, I ain't.
VIC:	C'mon, then.

(*As The Boy Comes Downstairs*)

VIC:	He's comin'. We'll just keep him on the go all day. Sade.
SADE:	All right, Vic. (*To The Boy*) How do you feel, Rush?

VICTOR: Fine, mom.

VIC: You won't feel so swell when I get you in the water. I'm gonna hold your head under for half an hour.

VICTOR: Y'can't do it!

VIC: Oh, can't I! C'MON!

VICTOR: C'mon, mom.

SADE: Coming, dear.

VIC: Last one in's a yella dog, and . . . (*Fade Out With Vic And The Boy Shouting Joyfully*)

    I got caught up in this show. I liked the script, liked what I had to do, and for the first time in my brief career I enjoyed acting. Perhaps because it didn't seem like acting; it was so natural and so much fun. And when it came time to break down I cried easily. I knew I was doing well. It was nothing like the acting I had done before. It was me. And perhaps it was easy to cry because I felt I was soon going to leave these people that I felt suddenly very close to and very fond of. In the rehearsal, I felt their acceptance, and, after the show, I had a sense that I might not be leaving after four days. And for some reason, I wasn't all that sorry.

Chapter Three

Paul Rhymer was born in Fulton, Illinois, in 1905. Shortly thereafter, his family moved to Bloomington, Illinois, where Paul went to elementary and high school. His childhood was on the lonely side. He had a brother, Elwood, a couple of years older, of whom he was very fond. But Ellwood was never well and died at thirteen. Paul's brother had a speech affliction, which caused him to speak in a stilted, formal manner as Rush often does later on.

Paul's father worked for the railroad and was away from home a good deal. During his early teen-age years, Paul was often left alone with his mother. A rather casual student, his principal pastime was attending movies with his mother or friends. He went practically every day, sometimes twice a day. His diary of this period reads like a compendium of the "B" pictures of this era. A typical entry would read: "Worked today, went to the movies—saw Lillian Gish in 'Lonely Hearts Aflame.'" There are pages and pages of entries exactly like this. It would seem to be the diary of a young man floating through life with hardly a thought in his head. But all this time those marvelously perceptive eyes and ears were storing impressions—and "Vic and Sade" was the result.

The high points of Paul's boyhood were the times he was with his father when they took the car on the "hard road" to Dwight or Moline. The relationship between Vic and Rush reflect this love. It's a relationship so full of good feelings, of fun, and the exploitation of the fun between father and son, it's tickling and delightful.

And the make-up of the family—the three characters, father, mother and son—paralleled Paul's own boyhood, and was significant for him. In any case, once Rush entered the show and the family was formed, it was as if some wellspring were touched in Paul and this storehouse of marvelous material poured forth. It was organic, and there was an incredible quantity. "Vic and Sade" was not like the other daytime shows in which a thin, elongated dramatic plot was advanced an iota each day. Each episode of Vic and Sade was a complete story, many of them intricate and ingenious, with a beginning, middle and end. There were six of them a week for several years and then five a week for a total of twelve years! The equivalent of about three hundred novels!

The scripts are the encyclopedia of the sights, the sounds, the feelings and the incidents—the minutiae of family life in a small town. It came from his memory, from perspective, from his projection of what it might have been and could have been, some from pure fantasy, but all of it had a foundation in truth.

Gradually, he was fleshing out and breathing life into his characters. He built them up out of a combination of real people (his parents and himself), the actors' personalities and proclivities and through experimentation with what he thought funny and worked. And always he weeded out those elements that seemed false and built the characters up bit by bit, molecule by molecule until they were wonderfully real and comic, larger than life, but so solidly fashioned that whenever he wanted to he could reach inside them for a feeling that spoke directly to the heart and guts of the listener.

But humor was always predominant. Paul saw things funny, and in constructing the characters the funny side was uppermost.

VIC: . . . I'm more the intellectual type. Love books . . . and literature and flowers . . . all that bunk.

SADE: Do you love flowers, Vic? I never noticed.

VIC: Oh, I don't know as I love 'em. I just sorta appreciate 'em. It's like that with all us spiritual cusses. I guess we feel things more than other people. Ya know, Sade, sometimes I feel like I wish I was more like you . . .

SADE: Like me?

VIC: Yeah, like you, Sade. There ain't much satisfaction in bein' a brainy type . . . Just keeps a fella keyed up, and on edge.

Sade, at the beginning, was very much the naïve country girl, painfully shy, who goes to pieces at the thought of the boss coming to dinner. She is also a romantic, constantly worried that Vic will tire of her, wants to kiss, wants Vic to reassure her. Paul got fun out of her lack of intellectual bent, but Sade slowly gained confidence and authority and became a forceful, Midwestern housewife; sometimes a martinet.

He knew his three principal characters down to their last ganglion. And they were complete characters, as delicately woven, complex, full of "wheels within wheels" as people are in life. We were always amazed at how a bachelor in his twenties had such knowledge of the inner workings of a thirty-three-year-old housewife, a middle-aged minor executive, and a twelve-year-old boy.

But he created besides a whole town full of characters . . . all the incidental people that Vic and Sade ran into during the course of their whimsical day. Mr. Gumpox, the garbage man; the Brick-Mush man; the gas meter reader; Mr. and Mrs. Croucher, who ran the grocery store; Hank Gutstop, the town bum; Harry Jamieson, the town imbecile; Reverend Cook; the later Reverend Kidneyslide; Mr. Chinbunny, principal of the school; Rush's friends: Smelly Clark, Fat Johnson, Heinie Call, Rooster Dave; Mr. Ruebush, Vic's boss; Sade's ladyfriends in the Thimble Club and hundreds more. And the incredible thing was that Paul gave each one of these people such a rich, full and unswerving personality, we could laugh at them because they behaved so characteristically.

And yet the audience heard only three voices—those of Vic, Sade and Rush. Paul used several devices to include these other characters, to make them a part of Vic and Sade's life and part of the show. There were one-sided telephone calls, so beautifully written you could imagine you heard what the other party was saying. Paul often got laughs from lines that were never said, only suggested, by our main characters' replies. We spoke to many of the people from the porch, on the street, in the alley or the backyard; we just never heard their answers. We talked about them at length, and so firmly were these people in Paul's mind that they became living, breathing people almost as much as our principal characters. And, as a matter of fact, many times these silent characters were the actual stars of the show!

One of Rush's early friends was Freeman Scudder, a deaf mute boy. Freeman could appear right on scene because he didn't speak. He communicated by writing on a pad he carried, and with gestures and facial expressions, usually interpreted by Rush. Paul sometimes wrote long scenes between Rush and Freeman, creating the illusion that two people were talking, when, of course, Rush was the only one to be heard. And like all the others, Paul made Freeman a very distinct personality. Freeman often drew pictures on his pad, and one day he sets about drawing a picture of Sade. But then, suddenly, for no apparent reason, he tears it up.

SADE: Why, Freeman! What's the matter? Why'd you tear up the nice picture you . . . Child, I . . . (***Stops Short: Pause***)

RUSH: I know why he tore it up, Mom.

SADE: Why?

RUSH: He couldn't a drawn you the way you looked just then . . . standin' there an' smiling. Nobody could. Ain't that right, Freeman? Sure . . . see, Mom?

And that was worth the price of admission for that day. Paul always gave you something in the last few lines to make it worthwhile. And often, in these first years, there was the love motif—of one of our family members for the other.

There was a dog, too, that Rush brings home one day. But of course, Paul couldn't have just an ordinary dog. This one was very special.

VIC: (***Still Fascinated By The Dog***) Doggone! I never seen an animal just like this one.

SADE: He's so . . . so stupid.

RUSH: No, he ain't.

SADE: Well, what's the matter with him?

RUSH: Nothin's the matter with him.

SADE: He just . . . stands there. An' looks. What's he lookin' at?

RUSH: I dunno. I guess he's lookin' at . . . (*To Dog*) Whatcha lookin' at, boy? The gas stove? Huh? Lookin' at the gas stove?

SADE: Hm.

VIC: Sade, did you ever see a chipmunk?

SADE: I don't think so.

VIC: I never did either. I wonder if this could be a chipmunk.

RUSH: (*Almost In Tears*) He's a dog. I tell ya. Won't ya please quit makin' fun of 'im.

SADE: We're not makin' fun of him, son. But . . . (*Giggles*) . . . what make him stand there like a statue?

VIC: Maybe he's dead.

RUSH: Aw.

VIC: He don't look like he's breathin'. An' he don't move a doggone muscle.

RUSH: Well, can't he stand still if he wants to!

VIC: Yeah, but . . . hey, look at him! For criminy sake!

SADE: (*Amazed*) He's . . . he's smilin'.

VIC: Doggoned if he ain't!

SADE: He is smilin'. (*Begins To Laugh: Vic Joins In*)

RUSH: Aw, how'd ya like to have somebody laugh at you?

❖ ❖ ❖ ❖

RUSH: I know I like him. He's a very unusual dog.

SADE: He certainly is.

VIC: He's the most unusual dog I ever saw.

SADE: Can't he bark even a little bit, Rush?

RUSH: Not even a yelp. He's a very silent dog.

SADE: Hm.

VIC: He's a very motionless dog too. Do you realize he ain't budged an inch?

SADE: Ain't even moved his foot.

RUSH: Well—he ain't goin' anywhere. He likes to stand nice an' still.

VIC: Is the reason he don't bark because he can't bark . . . or because he just don't want to bark?

RUSH: Aw, gov.

VIC:	I ain't foolin' with ya, son. Honest to gosh, I can't figure the pooch out at all.
RUSH:	He can't bark.
VIC:	How do ya know he can't?
RUSH:	He tries every once in a while. Nothin' comes out of his throat, though, except a kind of whoosh. Like this. (*Makes A Whoosh*)
VIC:	Hm.
SADE:	Well, can he . . . hey, look at him now.
VIC:	Son-of-a-gun!
RUSH:	(*Laughing*) Ain't he swell!
SADE:	He lifted his eyebrow!
RUSH:	Sure.
VIC:	Never seen such a thing.
SADE:	He—lifted—his—eyebrow. Just like a human.
RUSH:	Sure. He's a very unusual dog.
VIC:	He looks like he's surprised about somethin'.
RUSH:	He ain't, though. He just looks like he is.
SADE:	How do you know he ain't surprised, Rush?
RUSH:	I don't think anything ever surprises him.
VIC:	(*Laughs*) Aw.

RUSH:	Well, I don't.
SADE:	I don't either, Vic. Just look at that dog. Looks like he knew everything there was to know in the whole wide world.
RUSH:	(*Aff.*) Uh-huh. That's what I think.
SADE:	Well—looks like we got a new member of the family.
VIC:	Yes, sir, it sure does.
SADE:	What ya gonna call your dog, son?
RUSH:	Albert R. Johnson.
VIC:	Gonna call the dog that?
RUSH:	Sure. I made that name up myself.
SADE:	What a name to give a dog.
RUSH:	That's his name . . . Albert R. Johnson.
VIC:	But, shucks, son . . . (**Chuckles**) . . . people don't call dogs things like . . .
RUSH:	I know they don't, gov . . . but ya hafta figure on the dog when ya give him a name. I don't know no regular dog's name that would fit my dog.
SADE:	Why not? There's Spot . . .
RUSH:	He ain't go no spots.
SADE:	Well—Shep.

RUSH: That's a name for a collie.

VIC: Bowser.

RUSH: (*Disgusted*) Aw.

VIC: I guess Bowser ain't so good. (*Laughs*)

RUSH: I wouldn't name a horse Bowser.

SADE: Curly? No—he ain't so curly.

RUSH: Mom, he ain't curly at all.

SADE: No, he ain't. Well—Fido?

RUSH: Aw. (*Disgusted*) Fido.

VIC: Rover?

RUSH: Sissy name. Nope, his name is Albert R. Johnson.

SADE: (*Thoughtfully*) Albert R. Johnson.

RUSH: I think it kinda fits. This is a very unusual dog.

VIC: Doggone, Sade, I don't know but what he's right. Albert R. Johnson does kinda fit that mutt.

SADE: Why does it?

VIC: (*Laughing*) I dunno . . . but it does.

RUSH: Sure it does, mom.

SADE: Well—Albert R. Johnson is a very common name. You're liable to hurt somebody's feeling calling a dog that.

RUSH:	I don't think so, mom. Albert R. Johnson is a nice, sensible, solid, respectable kind of a name.
SADE:	Yes it is.
RUSH:	Well, this dog is that kind of a dog.
SADE:	Sensible, solid and respectable?
RUSH:	Yeah. Ain't he?
SADE:	I guess so. He don't look very frivolous.
VIC:	He sure don't. Looks sad.
RUSH:	Thoughtful, gov. He looks thoughtful.
VIC:	Doggone. He ain't moved yet.
RUSH:	He'll move. He just ain't got any reason for moving.
SADE:	Hm.
VIC:	An' his name is Albert R. Johnson.
RUSH:	Albert R. Johnson.
SADE:	That's a kind of a long name for a dog, ain't it, Rush?
RUSH:	Yeah. I'm gonna call him Mr. Johnson for short.
VIC:	Hello, there, Mr. Johnson.

(*Sound Effects: Whoosh*)

RUSH:	(*Laughs*) Well, whatcha think of that!

SADE: (*Laughs*)

VIC: Doggone!

RUSH: See, he knows his name already.

VIC: He sure does.

SADE: What d'ya know!

RUSH: An' he smiled when he said it.

SADE: An' lifted his eyebrow. (*Laughs*)

RUSH: Ain't he a fine dog!

SADE: I'm beginnin' to like him better. (*Laughs*) My—what a foolish dog.

RUSH: Mom, he ain't foolish. He's an unusual dog.

VIC: I hope to snort he is.

RUSH: Don't cha think you're gonna like 'im?

VIC: I anticipate a beautiful friendship between Mr. Johnson an' I. Yes sir.

SADE: Why don't cha walk him around a little bit, Rush?

RUSH: I think he'd rather stand still, Mom.

VIC: He ain't moved anything but his doggone eyebrow since he's been here.

SADE: It makes a person feel kinda peculiar to have a little dog around that stands still like a statue, an' just smiles.

RUSH: I'll walk 'im around for ya, Mom. C'mon, Mr. Johnson. C'mon.

VIC: Don't believe he's gonna do it.

SADE: No. I don't think he plans on moving.

RUSH: C'mon, Mr. Johnson. Walk!

VIC: Nope. He ain't gonna . . .

RUSH: (*Yells With Delight*) See!

SADE: C'mon, Mr. Johnson.

VIC: He even walks funny.

RUSH: He's a very unusual walking dog. This way, Mr. Johnson.

SADE: He walks so dignified . . . like he was goin' up to the altar to get married.

VIC: He sure don't hurry.

RUSH: Mr. Johnson can go faster if he wants to.

VIC: Darn, I still ain't sure about . . . I don't know much about dogs but all the dogs I ever seen looked like dogs.

RUSH: Gov, Mr. Johnson is a dog. I know he's a dog.

SADE: I guess he's a dog all right, Vic. See his tail.

RUSH: Sure. There y'are, Gov. Look at his tail. Ain't that a dog's tail?

VIC: Yeah, guess it is. There's somethin' funny about it at that, though.

RUSH: What's funny about it?

VIC: I dunno. It don't move.

RUSH: He could move it if he wanted to.

SADE: Looks like it'd been froze an' never got thawed out.

RUSH: No . . . it's a very warm tail. Feel it.

SADE: No. No, some other time.

RUSH: It's a very unusual tail.

VIC: Is there anything usual about that mutt? Hey . . . where's he goin'? Get 'im, Rush. Well, for gosh sakes!

SADE: (*Amazed*) He walked right into the table leg.

RUSH: Oh, Mr. Johnson . . . did ya hurt yourself? Gosh!

VIC: He walked right smack into it. With his head.

RUSH: I'll rub it for ya, Mr. Johnson. There, old boy.

SADE: Rush . . . he can't be a very smart dog. Run right into somethin' like that.

RUSH: He didn't mean to do it.

VIC: How are his eyes? Maybe he don't see good.

RUSH: He sees fine.

VIC:	But, thunder, dogs don't ram their heads into things like that.
RUSH:	Mr. Johnson was thinkin' about something. Heck, I've walked into buildings an' things myself when I was busy thinkin'.
SADE:	He didn't make a sound when he bumped his head. You'd think he'd squeal or somethin'.
VIC:	You would at that.
RUSH:	Some dogs might.
SADE:	Well . . . (*Sighs*) . . . I got to get dinner.
RUSH:	I get to keep the dog, don't I, Mom?
SADE:	I guess. But take him outside or down in the basement or somewhere now.
VIC:	Let's take him out on the porch, Rush. I wanta study him some more. The more I look at him the more I wonder what the dickens kind of a doggone thing he is.
RUSH:	C'mon, Mr. Johnson.
SADE:	Don't let him run into anything.
RUSH:	I won't, Mom.
VIC:	Be back in pretty quick, Sade.
SADE:	All right, Vic.
VIC:	C'mon, Mr. Johnson.
RUSH:	C'mon, Mr. Johnson.

On November 29, 1932, Freeman Scudder and Mr. Johnson were both in the script, so we had a large cast, with, however, no increase in the speaking parts. Freeman trades his corduroy pants for a third interest in Mr. Johnson and walks around with no pants on—funnier on radio than it would have been on TV.

A couple of days later, Rush tries to find out if Mr. Johnson is a bloodhound and lets the dog track him all over the house, but to give him a break Rush puts flour on his feet. In the next script Rush makes glasses for Mr. Johnson, also makes an eye chart, which is a picture of a bone. Gazing at it, Mr. Johnson says, "Whoosh!" and everyone is delighted.

Incidentally, I was the voice of Mr. Johnson, doing the "whoosh" which was his version of a bark, and also I was responsible for his demise, because one terrible day I couldn't seem to do the "whoosh" right and everybody was upset. The director came out of the control room and stood beside me while we were on the air, trying to get me back on the right track, but no matter how I tried, or perhaps because I got desperate, the "whoosh" got worse and worse. So Mr. Johnson disappeared.

The decision to have only three speaking characters was Paul's own. He did it, I guess, partly as a challenge, but also it worked greatly to his advantage in creating the very special world of Vic and Sade. Many of the people we knew were so strange and outrageous it would have been difficult to present them in tones of any human voice. Who would believe them? This way everyone could have their own image of Hank Gustop, Ike Kneesuffer, Fred and Ruthie Stembottom, Mis' Fisher—they were like characters in a funny dream, and it needn't be jarred by an actual voice. (It would have been a tough casting job too. Not to mention expensive.) But Paul used the peculiar strength of radio—its utilization of the listeners' imagination—and carried it a step further—double imagination, if you will—and allowed the audience to conjure up pictures of characters they never heard.

Today Mr. Gumpox's bride got into town! Vic comes home with the news. See, Mis' Kleeberger—Ike Kneesuffer's secretary—was down at the depot to meet her mother, and here was Mr. Gumpox taking a lady off the train. It's been well known that Gumpox has been writing to matrimonial agencies for years, and now it looks like he's found a wife! Sade is very excited. The phone rings and it's Mrs. Feeley up the street. When Sade finishes the conversation, her eyes are sparkling.

SADE: (*Hangs Up*) Vic, Mr. Gumpox an' his bride are comin' down the alley.

VIC: Yeah?

SADE: Just now passed Mis' Feeley's back yard. Oughta be by here in ten minutes or so.

VIC: Are they walkin'?

SADE: No, they're ridin'.

VIC: Well, that's a hot way to treat a new wife. Ride her down the back alley in a garbage wagon.

SADE: He's probably showin' her his route.

VIC: Shucks.

SADE: That's all right. Any new wife oughta be interested in her husband's work. Mis' Feeley says she's right handsome—near as she could tell from her kitchen window. Kinda fat—but real red in the complexion an' wearin' a nice cloth coat an' laughin' so jolly. Mr. Gumpox was laughin' too.

VIC: The happy bridegroom.

SADE: I'm gonna sit here in the window till they go past. Wouldn't miss it for a silver dollar.

VIC: We could throw some ol' shoes.

SADE: (*Pleased With The Notion*) Sure. An' we could . . .

(*Thinking Better Of It*) No, guess we better not. Mr. Gumpox might think we meant the old shoes for his garbage wagon. Hurt his feelins.

VIC: How'd it be to drape some orange blossoms around the garbage bucket an' . . .

SADE: (*Raps On Window*) Hi-tye-tye.

VIC: Gumpox an' spouse?

SADE: No, Rush.

VIC: Sade, how'd it be to drape some orange blossoms around the garbage bucket? That way we could convey delicate sentiments of best wishes an' happy . . .

SADE: Vic, don't you dare make fun of Mr. Gumpox if you happen to see him. He's been good to me an' . . . (*Door Opens*)

RUSH: (*Coming In*) Hey, guess who's comin' up the alley?

SADE: Mr. Gumpox an' a lady?

RUSH: (*Closing Door*) Yeah, an' ya know who the lady is?

SADE: Mrs. Gumpox.

RUSH: Yeah—how'd ya know?

SADE: Mis' Feeley just telephoned. Where are they?

RUSH: Just passin' Kane's house. Hi, Gov.

VIC: Hi.

SADE: You get a good look at the lady, Rush?

RUSH: Sure. I stood right beside the garbage wagon.

SADE: You say anything to Mr. Gumpox?

RUSH: Sure. An' he introduced me to his wife.

SADE: Really?

RUSH: I said, "Hello there, Mr. Gumpox." He said, "Hello, Rush, want you to meet Mrs. Gumpox." I said, "How do you do, Mrs. Gumpox?" She said, "Very well, thank you." Mr. Gumpox said, "Josephine, this is Rush Gook from down on Virginia Avenue. We'll be passin' his house directly."

SADE: Well. Josephine, huh?

RUSH: Yeah. He offered to give me a lift but there was no room on the seat an' I'd hafta ride back with the garbage so I declined.

SADE: You should of declined even if there was room on the seat. People that just got married like to be alone.

RUSH: That did cross my mind.

SADE: Was Mis' Gumpox fat?

RUSH: Oh, boy, I'll say. I liked her though. One of these kinda ladies that laugh easy, ya know?

SADE: Uh-huh.

RUSH: Ya know Mr. Gumpox got that wife just by writin' in to a mail order house?

SADE: Yes, I knew that.

RUSH: Pretty good system, seems to me. You take a guy all of a sudden feels like gettin' married: He whips out his fountain pen, sends his order in, an' by gosh on the next train here comes his good ol' wife.

SADE: Oh, it's not as simple as that. The people correspond first an' find out if they like each other. If they do, then they . . . Who's that in the alley?

RUSH: (*Looking*) Dirty Johnson an' his fish truck.

SADE: Say, Vic.

VIC: Uh-huh?

SADE: How'd it be to have Rush run out with the garbage bucket? It's not Mr. Gumpox's day, but if he sees it he'll stop an' take it. Give me a chance to get a glimpse of the bride.

VIC: Certainly O.K. by me.

SADE: That wouldn't hurt anything would it?

VIC: Guess not.

SADE: Rush, do that, will ya? Garbage bucket's beside the bottom step.

RUSH: Mom, I'm personally acquainted with Mrs. Gumpox. If ya want me to I'll notify her when she comes past you'd like to form her acquaintance an' . . .

SADE: No, that might look funny. Do like I say.

RUSH: (*Moves Off*) All right.

SADE: (*After Him*) An' I'd try not to let 'em see you.

RUSH: (*Opening Door*) O.K.

SADE: An' come back in yourself.

RUSH: Sure. (*Closes Door*)

SADE: (*To Vic*) I s'pose I'm pokin' my nose in other people's business doin' things like this, but I just can't help it. When somebody I know gets married, I get excited as a horse. Just like when somebody I know has a baby. Even when somebody I don't know has a baby an' I just hear about it, I hafta know all the details an' . . . (*Giggles*) Rush is puttin' the garbage bucket right out in the open where Mr. Gumpox can't miss it.

VIC: Poor ol' bridegroom Gumpox. He can't even take his wife out for a honeymoon ride on his garbage wagon but what somebody makes him stop for potato peelins'.

SADE: (*Tartly*) If that's the way you feel about it why didn't you say so when I asked ya.

VIC: (*Chuckling*) I take it back, kiddo.

SADE: Goodness, a person can . . . (***Door Opens: Raises Voice***) They comin'?

RUSH: Yeah.

SADE: Where are they?

RUSH: (***Closing Door***) Right by Harris'.

SADE: They see you?

RUSH: No.

SADE: Vic, c'mon, let's peek out the window.

VIC: (*Getting Up*) If the lady is lovely enough I don't know but what I'll step out an' ask to kiss the bride.

RUSH: Mom, ya know where Mr. and Mrs. Gumpox are gonna live?

SADE: No, where?

RUSH: 702 West Chestnut—little bungalow.

SADE: (*Approvingly*) Oh, that's good. Mr. Gumpox's told me several times he gets so tired of it there at the Bright Kentucky Hotel. Trains goin' by his window all night long.

VIC: Move over, folks. I, too, would love to see the wedding procession.

RUSH: It ain't come by yet.

SADE: (*Giggles*) I bet Mr. Gumpox stopped his horse there by Drummond's barn so they could have a little kiss.

RUSH: (*Laughs*) Mr. Gumpox an' his wife or Mr. Gumpox an' his horse?

VIC: (*Joins In This Laughter*)

SADE: Don't make a lotta noise now so they hear ya.

RUSH: Hey, Mr. Montgomery is garbage man over on Chestnut Street. I wonder if Mr. Gumpox plans on takin' his own garbage or do the professional rules state that . . . Here they come. Here they come.

VIC: If I was a bridegroom I think I'd pick out a horse for my wedding chariot that weighed at least ninety pounds an' could keep his head . . .

SADE: (*Delighted*) There's the bride. There's the bride.

VIC: Move over. Thunder.

SADE: Oh, she is a fatty. Wish she'd look this way once. Don't stick your head outa the curtain so they see ya, Rush.

RUSH: Well, heck, Gov's pushin' me in the back an' . . .

SADE: Mr. Gumpox sees the garbage. He's tellin' his horse to whoa.

RUSH: Hey, they have diamond weddings an' silver weddings an' golden weddings. Even have paper weddings. If they have garbage weddings I bet Mr. an' Mrs. Gumpox celebrate till who laid the chunk. I bet . . .

SADE: She's lookin' this way, Vic. She's lookin' this way.

VIC: Uh-huh. Not a bad lookin' dame.

SADE: She's a handsome woman. Just like Mis' Feeley said. (*Delighted*) Well.

VIC: (*Chuckles*) Hey, the ol' boy's showin' her how he handles garbage.

RUSH: He's puttin' on a demonstration.

VIC: Know what he's sayin'?

RUSH: What?

VIC:	Just a simple twist of the wrist.
RUSH:	(*Laughs*) Yeah, or else he's sayin . . .
SADE:	Vic, that's a real good cloth coat she's got on.
VIC:	Uh-huh.
SADE:	All her clothes show she's got refinement.
VIC:	Um.
SADE:	Look at her laugh at him. (*Giggles*)
VIC:	Um.
SADE:	Ain't that sweet?
VIC:	Um.
SADE:	Yes, sir, I believe Mr. Gumpox done all right. You can tell a nice person by their looks even from this distance.
RUSH:	Gov, I wish you'd get your elbow outa my back an' quit pushin' so I could . . .
SADE:	Stop that, will ya. Want them people to . . . They do see ya, Rush.
RUSH:	I couldn't help it, Mom. Gov's elbow.
SADE:	Mr. Gumpox is wavin'. Vic, open the window.
VIC:	Open it?
SADE:	Yes. Hurry up.

VIC: (*Opening It*) It's always my fault when things go wrong. I'm the poor unfortunate . . .

SADE: (*Calls*) Mr. Gumpox. Mr. Gumpox. Will you an' your wife come in the house a minute . . . an' . . . an' have coffee? Please do.

END OF SCRIPT

ANNOUNCER: Throw our congratulations and best wishes in your garbage wagon too, Mr. Gumpox. From what we've heard we gatheer you have taken unto yourself one dandy wife.

(*Pause*)

CLOSING AND COMMERCIALS

Chapter Four

My earliest recollection of Paul was standing behind him in the Continuity Department of NBC, watching him write a script. He typed very fast and I noticed there were a lot of broken speeches. I asked him if he knew how the sentences were going to end in his own mind. And he said no, he didn't.

The scripts of Vic and Sade are full of broken speeches, and Paul used them for comic effect, leaving your imagination to fill in something better left unsaid, or something that couldn't be said on the airwaves. Like the time Rush wanted to get tattooed by Link's uncle. He tells Gov all the things you can get tattooed for various prices, and then ...

RUSH: (*Laughing As He Goes*) Hey, Gov, for twenty five dollars you can get a steamboat tattooed on ...

VIC: (*With Mock Anger*) Get along with ya, or I'll come and get ya.

Paul cleverly circumvented censorship in several ways. One was by ending a speech at a strategic time; another was alluding to something so delicately you couldn't really be sure he meant what you were already laughing at, and the third was getting his scripts in so late. He always turned in his material so close to air time no one had a chance to read it before it was broadcast. Of course, no one was that concerned at first. The powers that be figured not enough people were listening to make a difference, and then when it was suddenly a hit they were reluctant to tamper with success.

Vic and Sade was about the simple joys of life. Vic asks Sade if she wants to walk part way to work with him, take a little early morning stroll. It sounds good. People were relaxed enough to take small pleasures. And it was about the joys of family life, written incidentally by a guy who was living almost the exact opposite sort of life himself at the moment. For, although the show was sustaining and practically unnoticed by the public, it was already recognized by people in the industry, at least around Chicago, and among Paul's associates he was looked upon as a very bright guy on the way up. So he was living the life of a bachelor with a future in the big city, a guy whose own life was pretty far from that of Vic and Sade.

It is an autumn night. Vic suggests a walk "down to the University and back." Sade accepts. It is one of those crisp nights with the smell of dead leaves and with a feeling of excitement in the air . . .

SADE: I guess I get the Halloween spirit before anybody else.

VIC: Oh, so that's it.

SADE: Maybe. It's something. Every year I get it. Twice a year I get it.

VIC: Get what?

SADE: Whatever it is. Youth maybe.

❖ ❖ ❖ ❖

SADE: Can you see my face?

VIC: Not very well.

SADE: Light a match and look at it.

VIC: I'll see if I got one. This seems kind of silly.

SADE: Got one?

VIC: Yeah. Here. (*Strikes Match*) Well, by gosh.

SADE: What do you see?

VIC: See a young girl . . . with bright eyes.

SADE: Sure you do.

VIC: What makes it?

SADE: September makes it, I guess. And the cold stars up there. And the wind. And the autumn darkness. And maybe you.

VIC: Me?

SADE: Sure.

❖ ❖ ❖ ❖

SADE: . . . And I stay in love with you year after year after year. And about twice a year that love . . . it just . . . just comes out on me . . . like chicken pox or something. And I get silly and my eyes get bright and I feel like walkin' pigeon-toed . . . like this.

VIC: Aw, you foolish kids. (*Chuckles*)

SADE: That's what I am . . . tonight. Tomorrow I'll get breakfast for you and Rush; fix the holes in Rush's pants; exchange recipes with Mis' Fisher over the back fence; and be every single minute of my thirty-four years. Vic . . . look how pretty the lights are in Sturdevant's window.

❖ ❖ ❖ ❖

SADE:	Vic . . .
VIC:	Yeah . . .
SADE:	Bet you're not game to ring a doorbell.
VIC:	Bet I am.
SADE:	C'mon then.
VIC:	Not old Calvert's doorbell. He's a tough monkey.
SADE:	C'mon. Don't be afraid.
VIC:	Old Calvert'll shoot us.
SADE:	No he won't. We'll run away like the wind. C'mon.
VIC:	Where is his darn doorbell?
SADE:	(*Whispering*) Here it is. Are ya ready to run?
VIC:	I'll say!
SADE:	Here goes! (*Rings Doorbell Violently*)
VIC:	Run, Sade!

END OF SCRIPT

Vic and Sade was full of the piddling details of living, ostensibly in a small town but, really, anywhere. It was cold, it was warm, it rained and it snowed; it was a bright day, a bleak day, a holiday, a day of disappointment. Changes of seasons and other transitions, birthdays and funerals, engagements and marriages, squabbles and warm moments of friendship. Wakings in the morning and going to bed at night. Waking up in the morning in a cold house, cold feet in bed, of Rush trying to crawl in bed with Vic and Sade. The talk of what's for breakfast and Paul evokes the whole feeling of what it's like to live in a small house in a small town with clean, pure air, frost on the window and all the warm nostalgia that goes with it.

Sade is in the kitchen, working, and Rush is in the living room. He yells for her to come in.

RUSH: Look!

SADE: Well, what do you know! Isn't that fine! Just look at that!

RUSH: You like the snow, don't ya, Mom?

SADE: Love it. Always did. Well, just look at that! Lands!

RUSH: Dandy big flakes, huh?

SADE: Gorgeous! Just look at that!

RUSH: Look at the snow here on the windowsill. Pretty, ain't it?

SADE: I should say! Look out, son, I'll hitch the curtain back.

RUSH: Kinda early for snow, ain't it, Mom?

SADE: A little bit, maybe. Kinda early for it to snow such big flakes anyway. See, Rush, how they sift down on the proch and then just disappear. (*Laughs*)

RUSH: There's Mr. Croucher's grocery boy 'cross the street.

SADE: Where? Oh . . . uh . . . huh . . . look at his cap.

RUSH: It's all over snow.

SADE: How'd ya happen to notice it was snowin', Rush?

RUSH: I heard some kids yellin' outside an' I got up off the floor to see who it was. And there was the snow. I was sure surprised.

SADE: I bet you were. Snow is always surprisin'. If a person actually thought about it they'd realize it was bound to snow sooner or later, but I don't know . . . snow sorta takes my breath away for a minute when I first see it.

A few days later Vic and Rush are carrying baskets of ashes out of the basement and out to the alley for Mr. Gumpox, the garbage man, to pick up. Rush sleepily sits down on one of the baskets, finds the ashes still warm and the experience sensual. He induces Vic to try it. Vic agrees: It's a good feeling.

RUSH: Uh-huh. If it was forty below zero, though, and a gentleman was sittin' out here, his face'd be freezing an' his . . .

VIC: Say, we oughta invite Mis' Donahue to come over and have a seat.

RUSH: O.K. (*Calls*) Mis' . . .

VIC: (*Chuckles*) Hey! No.

Sade finally comes out to see how they are doing, and after some talk they persuade her to try sitting in the warm ashes. She gives in and tries it. While they're sitting there, Gumpox goes by and they miss him.

There was lots of work to be done around the house. Cleaning the basement, the attic, putting up screens and taking them down, moving furniture, etc.

In housework Sade is the organizer and the whip; Vic and Rush are reluctant, especially Vic. Vic has a peculiar reaction to work around the house. At these moments he goes into something of a stupor, almost a coma, where his mind ceases to function.

One noontime, when the boys have finished their "dinner," Sade lead them outside and outlines a job she has for them—planting some Late Joe Butlers . . .

SADE: All right, I'll tell you how to do it. Scoop your holes three inches deep. Put one seed on each hole. Then fill in the dirt again.

RUSH: O.K.

SADE: An' put the holes about a foot apart.

RUSH: O.K.

SADE: An' make a nice even row.

RUSH: Yeah.

SADE: Hear all that, Vic?

VIC: (*Sluggishly*) Huh?

SADE: Hear what I said to do?

VIC: (*Sluggishly*) Scoop?

SADE: Show him, son. I hafta be gettin' in my dress. If there's anything you don't understand, just holler. I'll leave the window open.

RUSH: O.K., Mom. Here's your seeds, Gov.

VIC: Scoop?

RUSH: Huh?

Vic:	Time to scoop?
Rush:	I guess your mind is a million miles away.
Vic:	It is.
Rush:	Here's your seeds. Six of 'em.
Vic:	Thanks.
Rush:	I'm gonna sit on the cellar windowsill to scoop.
Vic:	Move over.
Rush:	You gonna sit down here too?
Vic:	Sure.
Rush:	We'll be in each other's way.
Vic:	What of it?
Rush:	(*To Vic*) I got one planted, Gov.
Vic:	Uh-huh.
Rush:	Gonna plant another one now.
Vic:	Uh-huh.
Rush:	Your hole's deep enough. Why don't you put the seed in?
Vic:	Seed?
Rush:	Sure. You got enough dirt scooped out.
Vic:	Oh.

RUSH: Darn funny name for flowers, ain't it—Late Joe Butlers? When ya read in the newspaper about the "late" somebody, it means he's dead. Maybe when Joe Butler died, some guy invented these flowers in his honor and called 'em "Late" Joe Butlers . . . Whatcha lookin' for?

VIC: Forgot what I done with my seeds.

RUSH: They're in your vest pocket.

VIC: Oh.

RUSH: Look: I'm finished with my second hole.

VIC: Yeah.

RUSH: It'd be just too bad if it was winter time an' we hadda plant these seeds. Ground'd be so hard a guy'd need dynamite to . . . Only one seed, Gov.

VIC: One?

RUSH: You put in three.

VIC: Only takes one, huh?

RUSH: Yeah, one seed gives one Late Joe Butler.

VIC: (*Sighs*) Oh, my.

RUSH: (*Laughs*) You don't like this kinda work very well, do ya?

VIC: No.

But trying to convey the essence of the show in a book is tough. It came to its audience day by day in "brief interludes," and therein, to a great extent, lay its charm, like daily visits from familiar and welcome friends.

Perhaps it might help to give some idea of the real flavor of the show if I present a few of the plot lines, along with some notes I took as I went over the scripts:

#52	Rolling snowballs—These early scripts had the same sense of fun as *The Katzenjammer Kids* of that era—Everything was fun—all sorts of childish mischief. V & S joined in. Now people are too serious for that kind of thing. Real fun. Getting ready for big snowball battle. Vic helps Rush, gets caught in battle.

Jan. 1 '33	Rush complains nothing to do New Year's Day. Sade says it's a great day to have fun—the three together. Vic gets call—something doing at Plant and the boys'll go to the Greek's afterward. Rush gets call from friend—Uncle (ventriloquist) is coming over—Both start out happy, then realize Sade will be alone. Both go back. This is a beautifully and deceptively engineered script and does a lot in 15 minutes.

Jan. 1	R & V feet in hot water.

Jan. 11	First mention of Mildred Tisdel—Rush's girl. Rush's got himself in a spot where he's got to sell 130 tickets to hear a fella sing Chinese songs. Midwestern idea that foreigners are funny.

Jan. 21	Sade sneaks Rush into bed with her and Vic. She comes into his room to close window—it's raining at night—familiar.

Jan. 30	Raining. Sade's gonna make fudge. A man they knew did away with himself—with a pick axe, of all things.

Jan. 31   Rush has bad cold—Sade wants him to take medicine. Sings to him. Vic comes home with Ruebush—finds them both asleep—they go to restaurant.

Paul writes such great stuff for actors—the rapid-fire contrapuntal stuff that so perfectly illustrates a mood—pgs. 5 & 6 Sade's nervousness at Vic's having to make his first speech in a tux. "Dress Suit."

VIC: I'll just put the hat on the table, and . . .

SADE: No, no, no. Don't touch that hat.

VIC: Criminy!

SADE: Oh, Vic, you act like such a child.

VIC: Where'm I gonna sit down?

SADE: Do you hafta sit down?

VIC: You said I should sit down.

SADE: Do you have to have somebody to tell you to sit down?

VIC: No, I don't have to have nobody to tell me to sit down.

SADE: Well, stand up then and . . . Look out, Vic!

VIC: What's the matter?

SADE: Thought you were gonna knock that shirt off the chair.

VIC: Gosh, you'd think I was gonna go to Europe the way . . .

RUSH: (*Coming In*) Here's the shoes. Ain't they shiny?

VIC: Ya did a good job, son. Give 'em here.

SADE: No, no. Rush, what ya goin' to do with them shoes?

RUSH: Give 'em to Gov.

SADE: No, no. Give 'em here.

RUSH: Here they are, Mom.

SADE: Well, what do I want with 'em? Set 'em down.

RUSH: Where?

SADE: Anywhere. Lands, (**Brushing Coat**) how lint and stuff does stick to dress coats. That's because they're so glossy and . . . Rush, what are you doin' with them shoes?

RUSH: Settin' 'em down here.

SADE: Well, don't set 'em down there. First thing ya know, somebody'll trip over 'em, an' you'll have to polish 'em all over again.

RUSH: Where shall I set 'em down?

SADE: Set 'em down . . . set 'em down . . . I don't know. Set 'em down anywhere. Cantcha see I'm busy?

RUSH: How about under the davenport?

SADE: All right. All right. Lands, I never seen such a boy . . . Can't figure out where to set a little pair of shoes.

VIC:	(*Chuckling*) Not such a little pair of shoes, Sade. Biggest pair of shoes in this . . .
SADE:	Lands, why don't this lint come off the collar? (*Brushing*) What'd you say, Vic?
VIC:	I said, "Not such a little pair of . . .
SADE:	Rush, what'd you do with them shoes?
RUSH:	Set 'em under the davenport.
SADE:	Well, what a fine place to set a pair of shoes. You mighta gone away an' we'd never a found 'em.
RUSH:	You said . . .
SADE:	Why dontcha go play?
RUSH:	O.K. Have a good time at the Luncheon Club, Gov. I'll be out in front when ya go by in your dress suit . . . (*Fading*)
SADE:	Where you goin', Rush?
RUSH:	Goin' over to Seymour's vacant lot.
SADE:	Oh, no, you're not. You're gonna stay right here and help.
RUSH:	But you said . . .

These scripts were broadcast as they came out of typewriter, no rewrites. Not like television scripts today that might be rewritten 10 times by 4 or 5 different hands before they are shown. All you need is one genius!

Feb. 24   Mr. Hulsizer got hit by a train—died.

March 3, Page 3

VIC: The poet Whittier said, "Be leisurely in your eating always, but be most leisurely when eating peaches."

SADE: What'd he mean by that?

VIC: Just what he says.

Couldn't do that in TV now. Standards and Practices would send note: "Be sure this quote from Whittier is correct."

Marked scripts (by actors). Vic made a mark like this: VIC: under his lines. Sade and I marked scripts with straight line. Bern and I were kind of allied against Van.

Lots of scripts along in here about cleaning the house, sweeping walks, doing chores where Sade is organizer and task master. Vic and Rush loaf and digress.

March 8 (originally Sept. 22, 1932. Paul must have taken a vacation here.) Rush gets up at 5 to exercise, keeps Vic from sleeping.

This form was perfect for Paul. With all this writing he had to have characters stand around and stall a lot—and he could write the funniest stalling language in the world.

March 9 (originally Nov. 12, '32) They're gonna put up a family for the night—Seven people in a pair of twin beds—a big gang—the arrangements. Took the trials of ordinary family and carried them to outrageous lengths.

He was a master of idle chatter. So many of these scripts are concerned with the day-to-day activities of an ordinary family in a small town—the moments—Paul doesn't miss any—explored them all—the good feelings—the funny ones—the poignant ones, the warm ones. Did it with such charm . . . tickles you. Just along the way he drops in a delightful touch here and there:

SADE: Awful dark out, isn't it?

RUSH: Gee, yes. This is the darkest evening I ever saw.

SADE: (*Correcting Him*) Seen.

RUSH: Seen. Whatch doin' to the iron, Gov?

And it's dropped—no one ever mentions that Sade is wrong. Rush accepts his Mother's verdict and that's that—and Paul tells us a lot in a second or two. Rush is always wanting to get in bed with Vic and Sade—Charming scenes.

May 31   (orig. Dec. 29, '32) Vic and Rush playing checkers in kitchen while Sade fixes cranberries at sink.

June 1   (orig. Oct. 12, '32) Rush and Sade—Rush comes in in a hurry to get catcher's mitt. Sade is making a shirt for Rush on machine. Wants him to try it on. In his impatience calls it a "rotten" shirt. Spends rest of script being sorry—finally convincing Sade it's a wonderful shirt. Conscious of all the sights and sounds of small town—recreates them to bring 'em back.

June 7   (orig. Jan. 7, '33) Somebody parks a great long car in alley. Vic, Sade and Rush are fascinated—look at it. Vic and Rush honk horn accidentally, get in, get all mixed up with it. Sade is embarrassed.

Paul always had a thing with cars. Vic and Sade never got one. It was a class thing with them. A separation of classes by who owned automobiles and who didn't. Vic and Sade didn't.

June 8   Rush is oiling chains on bicycle. Vic sits down, watches him oil his bike. Box of candy is delivered to Sade—Rush inveigles Vic step by step into eating a lot of it.

CHAPTER FOUR | 83

June 14	Vic and Rush don't want to go in house because Sade has the ladies over. Rush is afraid fat Mrs. Wilcox'll want to kiss him as she usually does. He goes up on porch and Mrs. Wilcox, in the kitchen for a glass of water, catches him and kisses him. Vic comes up on porch. They see ice cream freezer, begin dipping fingers in it, then an old envelope. Sade comes out and catches them.
Jun 15	Rush buys present for mother—big pink pearls from Link's sister, Stevedora—Sade is shocked at sight of them—vulgar—Then Rush tells how they have nothing to eat at Link's house. The $8 will help a lot. Sade pretends to love pearls.
June 16	Sade cuts Rush's hair, gets bowl stuck on his head.
June 17	First time cleaning the attic. Vic, Sade and Rush.
June 21	Lock themselves out early in morning in night clothes. People coming along alley laugh at them.
June 29	Sade and Vic sit out on back porch steps. Sade wants to look at the moon. Vic talks about their garbage bucket. What a great, serviceable garbage bucket it is.
July 3	Sade is reading items from Carlock paper—This is a device Paul used frequently—reading items from paper.

When the script was short Paul would write a page or two more as insert—usually a yarn about some outrageous person or thing they did. The following is a typical insert.

The script began with Sade coming to Rush's room to wake him up in the morning, but it was a minute or so short, so Paul went down the hall to his office and wrote this insert.

SADE: Here's your underwear. Hurry up and get into it.

RUSH: Mom, how do they make underwear?

SADE: How do they make it?

RUSH: Yeah. How do they . . . (*Yawns*)

SADE: I dunno. S'pose they . . . I don't know. Machine, I s'pose.

RUSH: Sewin' machine?

SADE: I expect. Here, give me your pajamas.

RUSH: Here's the pants.

SADE: You're sittin' on the coat. Up.

RUSH: (*Chuckles*) Squirt was tellin' me how you can send away for underwear. He read it in a magazine. All ya hafta do is . . .

SADE: Here's clean stockin's on the chair

RUSH: Um.

SADE: What was it about Squirt?

RUSH: He read about a place where you can send away for underwear. (*Laughs*) You sent 'em your size and they send you the underwear.

SADE: What's so funny about that?

RUSH: They had a real funny way of havin' ya send in your size. You're supposed to put some water in your bathtub, an' make a mark where the water comes to, an' then you get in the bathtub, an' make a mark where the water comes to then.

SADE:	(*In Disbelief*) No.
RUSH:	(*Laughing*) Wait, I ain't through tellin' it. After ya got the two marks in the bathtub, ya put the bathtub in a crate or somethin' an' send it to the underwear factory. An' they figure out your size an' send you your underwear.
SADE:	(*Laughing*) Never heard anything so ridiculous.
RUSH:	Funny thing, huh?
SADE:	Squirt figure that out?
RUSH:	No, he read it in a magazine. An' he . . . (*Laughs*) if ya don't want to send in the bathtub, there's another way to get your size.
SADE:	What's that?
RUSH:	Well—ya fill the bathtub clean up to the top an' then you get in the bathtub, an' you catch the water that spills over, an' send that in. If you want loose fittin' underwear, all ya gotta do is add more water.
July 26	Introduction of Steve Chestbutter. Vic's golf clothes.
July 28	Sade is fixing Rush a picnic basket to take Sidney Call to a picnic.
Sept. 21	First time Vic calls Rush by any other than real name.
RUSH:	Hello.
VIC:	How do, Pontiac.

From September 15, 1933, scripts say Jelke Co. (We now have a sponsor! But it didn't last long.)

These are great scripts. Paul hitting on all four. I was recommended by Van. (Van Harvey was a friend of my father—used to patronize my father's tavern.) But Menser had heard of me too—not many child actors around—I think I may have been the only one available.

Oct. 4   Man at door—selling brick mush. Brick mush man later became a regular character mentioned. Rush breaks a window with football: Rush finds a horse. First mention of Mr. Kneesuffer. They say hello to him in alley.

Oct. 12   Taking down porch swing—Paul signaled seasons with this.

Oct. 14   Vic trying to do work at home—everybody bothers him.

Oct. 19   Sade and Vic worry about telling Rush he needs to have tonsils out. Then find out that's what he wants for Christmas.

Oct. 21   About to leave for the hospital. Wants to exploit operation. Shocked at having to go on streetcar. Wanted ambulance—Printed sign and everything. Invited 45 kids to see operation. Then learns two other kids from class are going to have tonsils out the same day.

Paul's humor was designed for the ear. I suppose this was partly because his career started in radio and developed there, but partly it was his own predilection. Had he been born a little later and worked in television, perhaps his writing would have developed along more visual lines. But I can't help but believe that radio was perfect for the sort of humor that came most easily to him.

Nov. 2, '33:

RUSH: (*Giggles*) Naw. I mean ya know why we say Santy Claus?

VIC: No.

RUSH: We had it in school today. We got it from the French people.

VIC: Got what?

RUSH: The name Santy Claus. Ya know what Santy Claus is in French?

VIC: No.

RUSH: Saint Nicholas . . .

VIC: Saint Nicholas, huh?

RUSH: Yeah, an' the way ya say it in French is "Sen Nickola."

VIC: So?

RUSH: Yeah, I'll show ya how it works. Keep sayin' Sen Nickola over an' over again an' pretty soon you'll catch yourself sayin' Santy Claus.

VIC: Will I?

RUSH: Yeah. Try it. Say Sen Nickola over an' over.

VIC: (*Says It, Finally Saying Santy Claus*)

RUSH: (*Pleased*) See?

VIC: (*Chuckles*) Uh-huh.

RUSH: Pretty good, huh?

VIC: Yeah. But you can do the same thing with Murphy.

RUSH: How ya mean?

VIC: Keep sayin' Murphy over to yourself an' pretty soon you'll catch yourself sayin' Indianapolis.

RUSH: Aw.

VIC: Try it.

Nov. 25 — Rush and Vic have to take out ashes again. The vanity of Mis' Fisher—never speaks but Paul paints the perfect picture of the neighbor you're afraid of—always looking out the window—finicky about yard, always sense her monumental disapproval. Kicked football into her yard. She's always looking out when Vic is behaving foolishly. Or when family is doing something reprehensible. She is the censor of small town society. The arbiter of correct behavior. The proprieties. Finally break Mis' Fisher's window.

Nov. 28 — Mr. Ruebush sends Rush a wagon for Christmas that cabinet maker in shop made. It's for little kid. Sade decides to send it to Bess and Walter's twins. The wagon is beautiful. Rush takes it outside, comes back, breaks down and cries—for his vanished childhood.

Dec. 2 — Paul's dialogue is so sharp and real—practically leaps off page—because characters' thoughts are so carefully denoted—each thought is caught—in proper sequence—it is startling. Dialogue seems to go faster than man can type—as fast as thought itself—either Paul was lightning typist or he could retain these flashes and hold them till he got 'em down on paper.

Dec. 18   Vic comes to Rush's bed to get warm. You can feel the cold in their dialogue. Vic wants to sleep—Rush keeps talking—of course, someone had to keep talking or there'd be no show—but the way Paul does it—it's funny and seems justified. He makes the necessity of dialogue funny. Often sets up a necessity of silence—of course, there can't be silence—but the breaking of the silence is comic. He makes audience laugh just because character speaks—instead of character having to force speech on listener's ear. Keeps promising silence—but you know there can't be silence.

Jan. 2, '34   First mention of Heinie Call—brother of Sidney.

SADE: (*To Rush*) Eat all your egg now. Don't leave good yella in the bottom of the cup.

The kind of homey tidbits that used to make Bern laugh at rehearsal—rip a laugh out of her as she said the line for first time. And the recollecting ear of Paul for that kind of shit—amazing!

One of Paul's great abilities, that was often remarked upon and that made it possible for him to do a show like this (a different story each day for so many years), was that he could take a seemingly trivial situation and make it the basis for a script. Digging fish worms in the yard, cleaning the house, being home sick with a cold, roasting potatoes in the alley, the recounting of a chance remark, a wash rag sale at Yamilton's . . . Paul could often get half a script out of a rummy game or checker game between Vic and Rush and make it interesting and amusing.

He did it by not missing anything; He hurried over nothing. Each and every moment to Paul was wotchy of attention, and he himself could derive pleasure from the tiniest and most insignificant things. He got more fun from taking a ride in the country with the top down or chatting with a friend than most people get from a wild party. He was interested and curious about everything and he approached each moment of his life with a completely open and receptive attitude. He was aware of all the components of a moment—the look, the sound, the emotional content—and he exploited all this in the scripts of Vic & Sade. Something that would take an instant to relate for an ordinary writer, or perhaps seem too inconsequential to bother with at all, Paul would explore in detail, lovingly, thoroughly, exhaustively. And when he ran across a comic vein, he worried it like a terrier and wouldn't let go until he'd gnawed all the juice and substance out of it.

He had the courage to really look and see, to listen and hear. Most of us are so busy protecting ourselves from hurt that we're afraid to really look and listen, but Paul wasn't. Perhaps because he somehow avoided the early childhood traumas—being unobtrusive and in every way a part of the accepted group—so that he was never gun-shy of the emotional wounds that make so many of us draw on a thick skin.

Nov. 22, '32.

RUSH: (*Excitedly*) Hey, Mom!

SADE: What is it?

RUSH: Look!

SADE: Where?

RUSH: Comin' up the street!

SADE: My lands!

RUSH: Whose funeral is it?

SADE: Must be that Mr. Robinson that died.

RUSH: Mr. Robinson over on Cedar Avenue?

SADE: Yes. Did you know him?

RUSH: Sure. Freeman an' me raked up his leaves for him 'bout a month ago. Gee whiz, is he dead? He was just a young fella. Had the nicest . . .

SADE: Oh, no. That's his son. The Mr. Robinson that died was a very old man . . . pretty near eighty, I think I read in the paper.

RUSH: Did he live over on Cedar Avenue, too?

SADE: Ye-es . . . yes, he did. I know because . . . my lands! Look at all the cars. He musta had a lotta friends. Look, Rush, see 'em turning clear over on University?

RUSH: Yeah. Gee, this is gonna be fun!

SADE: (*Reproachful*) Rush!

RUSH: Oh, Mom, I didn't mean that. I meant . . . well . . . the funeral's goin' right by the house an' it's such a big one . . . an' . . .

SADE: I know what you mean, Rush. It is nice to watch the pretty automobiles.

RUSH: They go so slow, don't they?

SADE: Uh-huh.

RUSH: Oh, I remember the man that's dead. I bet.

SADE: You do?

RUSH: Yeah. When me'n Freeman got through rakin' the

leaves that day, Mr. Robinson invited us in the kitchen to have a glass of cidar.

SADE: Yes, I remember you said that.

RUSH: Well, when we got in the kitchen, there was a real old man sittin' by the window. Real nice old man, too. Cracked some jokes, an' showed us some tricks with matches.

SADE: Uh-huh. That was Mr. Robinson all right.

RUSH: He let Freeman draw a picture of him.

SADE: Did he?

RUSH: Yeah . . . an' he . . . oh, gee, Mom, aren't the automobiles shiny an' nice?

SADE: Yes. I wonder . . . if we . . .

RUSH: What, Mom?

SADE: I wonder if we oughta go in the house.

RUSH: Why?

SADE: Maybe it'd show . . . show more respect. Maybe we oughtn't ought to stand an' stare while the funeral goes by.

RUSH: I . . . I'd hate to miss it, Mom.

SADE: (*Laughing A Little*) Oh, son. Maybe we had better go inside . . .

RUSH: Mis' Fisher's peekin' outa her front curtains.

SADE:	Is she?
RUSH:	Yeah.
SADE:	Well, I think it shows just as much respect to sit out on the porch an' watch respectful as it does to peek through curtains.
RUSH:	Can we stay then, Mom?
SADE:	Yes, But don't feel like it was a circus parade goin' by, son . . . You . . . (*Giggles A Little*) . . . just can't keep the pleasure from showin' in your face.
RUSH:	I don't mean to be like that, Mom.
SADE:	No, of course you don't. You're just young an' . . . Rush, dontcha think we oughta put the swing back up before the automobiles get here? We don't want to stand here . . .
RUSH:	We could sit on the steps.
SADE:	No-o. No, h'ist up quick, son.
RUSH:	Yeah. (*Jumps Up*)
SADE:	Be careful now.
RUSH:	Yeah, Mom. Got a-hold of the swing?
SADE:	Yes. Go ahead n' hook it.
RUSH:	(*Grunts*) There!
SADE:	Come down now.
RUSH:	(*Jumping Down: Laughs*) We did a real quick job . . .

SADE: Be quiet, Rush, the cars are pretty near . . . (*Calls Restrainedly*) . . . Hello, Mis' Gilwee.

RUSH: (*Like Sade*) Hello, Mis' Gilwee.

SADE: (*Whispering Maybe*) Hurry an' sit down, son.

RUSH: (*Whispering*) Yeah, Mom.

SADE: Oh, lands, what a beautiful hearse.

RUSH: I seen it before. What color is it?

SADE: It's . . . (*Softly And Sweetly*) . . . How do you do, Mis' Klemm.

RUSH: Hello, Mis' Klemm.

SADE: (*Whispering*) Oh, I bet Mis' Klemm don't know what to do?

RUSH: Whatcha mean, Mom?

SADE: The funeral caught up with her, an' she didn't know it. Now she's gotta walk along beside the procession.

RUSH: I bet she's embarrassed.

SADE: I bet she is. Why don't she turn in somewhere?

RUSH: She can't turn in at Mis' Fisher's, can she?

SADE: Why can't . . . oh, they're on the outs.

RUSH: Yeah . . . An' there won't be another house to turn into till she gets to Mulvaney's.

SADE: She shoulda turned in here.

RUSH: There goes Mr. Stembottom's car, Mom.

SADE: Which one?

RUSH: The one with the . . . the one right in front now.

SADE: Ye-es, I believe that is, Fred an' Ruthie's car.

RUSH: That's Harry Kirby drivin'.

SADE: Who?

RUSH: Harry Kirby. Works down at the ice plant.

SADE: Hum, musta borrowed the car.

RUSH: Yeah.

SADE: Rush, look at that monstruous big auto. Oh, my! That's the loveliest . . . What kind of car is that?

RUSH: I dunno. Never seen one like it before. Gee, it's big, ain't it?

SADE: Pro'bly belongs to some of the people that came down from Chicago to go to the funeral. I read in the paper that Mr. Robinson had lotsa friends in Chicago that was . . . Rush, there's Mr. and Mrs. Donahue.

RUSH: Where?

SADE: In the blue sedan . . . right by the . . .

RUSH: Uh-huh. Are we gonna wave?

SADE: Wave? Why, I don't—think—so.

RUSH: They see us.

SADE: Uh-huh . . . but they ain't wavin'. I don't believe . . .

RUSH: They're noddin', Mom.

SADE: Well, then . . . maybe we better nod.

RUSH: Shall I nod now, Mom?

SADE: Yes, go ahead. An' I'll . . . (*Giggles A Little As She Nods; Almost Under Her Breath*) Hello, Mis' Donahue . . . (*Giggle*)

RUSH: Mr. and Mis' Donahue are sure dressed up, ain't they? I never seen 'em look so swell before.

SADE: Yes, they look awful nice.

RUSH: (*Loud Whisper*) Hey, Mom! Here comes Bulldog Drummond on his bicycle.

SADE: Well, let him go on by. Don't say anything to him.

RUSH: All right.

SADE: Rush!

RUSH: Yeah, Mom.

SADE: There's the minister . . . Reverend Garner.

RUSH: Uh-huh. Doggone!

SADE: Those people in the car with him must be some of the Robinson family.

RUSH:	Yeah . . . they all look sad, don't they?
SADE:	Yes. Oh, I do feel so sorry for people at a time like this. They go through so . . . Rush, isn't that young Mr. Robinson there in the big black car?
RUSH:	Yeah . . . yeah . . . that's him.
SADE:	An' I suppose that old lady's his Mother.
RUSH:	I dunno. Maybe. I never seen her.
SADE:	Pro'bly is, poor old soul. Wonder why it is they got the mourners so far from the hearse. Guess it's a new fashion.
RUSH:	Yeah.

(*Pause*)

RUSH:	That's all the funeral, Mom.
SADE:	Yeah.
RUSH:	It was kinda fu . . . interesting, wasn't it?
SADE:	(*Laughs At Him A Little*) Yes, I suppose it was.

(*Pause*)

RUSH:	Shall we take the swing down now, Mom?
SADE:	Yeah . . . guess we better.
RUSH:	(*Sighs*)
SADE:	(*Sighs*) Well—h'ist up on the rail.

Rush: O.K.

Sade: An' be careful. You don't wanta go an' break your leg with Christmas just a little over a month away an' . . .

End of Script

Chapter Five

SADE: (*On Phone*) . . . Yes, I suppose it is funny. Well, call again when you've stopped laughing. 'Bye, Ruthie. (*Hangs Up*) Oh, Vic . . .

VIC: What is it?

SADE: It's Rush.

VIC: What's he done?

SADE: He's gone into business. (*Laughs*)

VIC: Business?

SADE: Yes. Do you know what he did with those shoes of yours?

VIC: Of course I don't. What'd he do?

SADE: He didn't take 'em upstairs at all. He took 'em over to Link's house.

VIC: The colored lad?

SADE: Yes. An' from what Ruthie says he got Link's three big brothers . . . they're all big black giants, you know . . .

VIC:		Yes, yes.
SADE:		He's got those three colored men to break in your shoes.
VIC:		No.
SADE:		Yes! And they're paradin' around town that way!
VIC:		Great guns!
SADE:		Ruthie says the three colored men are walking abreast down the middle of the street . . .
VIC:		With my shoes on!
SADE:		Yes, with your shoes on. And Ruthie says she's never seen anything funnier in her life. Those men are so big and black and their shoes are so big and yella.
VIC:		My shoes you mean.
SADE:		But that isn't the worst! Rush himself is walking in front of the parade carrying a sign.
VIC:		(*Scared*) What's the sign say, Sade?
SADE:		I don't know exactly. Ruthie couldn't make it all out. Something about "The Shoes you see belong to Victor Rodney Gook, Chief Accountant of the Bookkeeping Department of the . . ." oh, all that, you know.
VIC:		Yes . . . for gosh sakes, what else does it say?
SADE:		Oh, something about if you have any shoes you want broke in just send 'em to Rush and he'll get his Professional Shoe-Breakers to break 'em in for you.

VIC: (*Makes A Sound Of Utter Defeat*)

SADE: That accounts for Mr. Croucher and that Mr. Wheadon actin' so funny.

VIC: Sade, that boy has gone too far this time. Lordy, what's this going to do to me?

SADE: It won't do any special harm, will it?

VIC: It'll make me the laughingstock of the town, that's what it'll do.

SADE: Oh, I wouldn't worry . . .

VIC: Wouldn't worry! Sade, I've got to go head them guys off . . . (*Phone*) Don't answer it, Sade. Some smart-aleck wants to know . . .

SADE: Hello . . . oh, hello, Mr. Bucksaddle . . . yes . . . yes . . . they are! . . . can you still see 'em? Thanks, Mr. Bucksaddle. (*Hangs Up*) Vic, they just went by the house, Mr. Bucksaddle says. C'mon, let's run to the window.

VIC: Oh, thunderation, I . . .

SADE: Oh, look, Vic! (*She Laughs*) See 'em.

VIC: (*In Despair*) Oh!

SADE: (*Laughing*) Look at all those yella feet . . . all keepin' time. And look at that sign. And look at Rush strut!

VIC: Oh.

SADE: And look at the neighbors! Everybody's out on

	their front porch watchin'! Vic, you can't wear those shoes after this!
VIC:	(*Stirring, To Himself*) Sade, go after 'em. Stop 'em!
SADE:	I couldn't do that, Vic. You wouldn't have me running up the street after three colored men, would you? You go!
VIC:	And have all the neighbors see me! Sade, I'll never live this down . . . never!
SADE:	Well, they're almost out of sight now. If you're gonna catch 'em, you'll have to hurry. You better go, Vic. You don't want 'em to get down to the business section of town.
VIC:	But, Sade . . . Oh, I guess I gotta go all right . . . (**Phone**)
SADE:	Hello . . . oh, hello, Mr. Ruebush . . . yes, he's here . . . Vic!
VIC:	Yeah. Hello, Mr. Ruebush . . . yeah . . . what? . . . what am I trying to do? . . . well, lemme tell ya, Mr. Ruebush . . . the way of it is . . . what? . . . everybody in town knows those are the kind of shoes you wear? . . . well, Mr. Ruebush, it was like this . . . ya see, I . . . now, don't be sore, Mr. Ruebush . . . no . . . no, I ain't tryin' to pull nothin', Mr. Ruebush. Now, listen, Mr. Ruebush . . . (*Into Theme*)

END OF SCRIPT

In the next day's script Vic and Rush are walking together, one to school, the other to work:

Vic:	Sure I'm mad about yesterday. Wouldn't you be mad if somebody took three pairs of your best shoes—shoes worth eighteen dollars a pair—and gave 'em to three colored fellas so's they could parade around the streets?
Rush:	I didn't think, Gov. When I got the idea of havin' Link's brothers break in your shoes for you, I thought it was the swellest idea in the world.
Vic:	Well, it wasn't a bad idea, son . . . showed a lot of cleverness on your part. And I gotta hand it to ya, you certainly put on a show for the town. The way you had them fellas marchin' down the street keepin' time was great!
Rush:	Gee, Gov, I thought you were mad.
Vic:	I was mad yesterday, Rush. That sign you were carrying with my name on it . . . well, I expect folks'll kid me about that until I'm an old man.
Rush:	And you're not gonna lick me or nothin'?
Vic:	No, son. I couldn't very well, could I? You haven't been bad. You've been thoughtless and impulsive and just a little cruel . . . but you haven't been bad. Swell guy I'd be if I punished you.

And so Rush receives the gentle indoctrination into the proper attitudes for a little WASP boy in Central Illinois, probably much as Paul himself got it.

This went on network radio in 1932 and was therefore acceptable to network sensibilities at that time. But even then, though I hardly admitted it to myself, this kind of thing bothered, me, being a little Jewish boy myself.

But—and this may be difficult to conceive—this was presented as enlightened thought, as the networks always try to do. It was liberal thought in the Midwest at that time. Paul was a sophisticated Midwesterner, after all.

And, given his background, there was yet a special thing operating with Paul. To him, black people were a phenomenon with comical aspects. As almost every person alive was to him a phenomenon with comical aspects. Paul viewed it all with the frank interest of a child who might go up to a black man and ask if his penis is black too—to the shock and horror of his mother. Or like my own fourteen year old boy, who says out loud the things most people think but don't say. In many ways Paul viewed the world like a fourteen-year-old boy. And expressed himself the same way.

Paul was open about his attitude toward blacks because he saw nothing wrong in it. It was an accident of nature. There was perhaps some stigma attached to it, but that's life. He never considered that perhaps colored people felt bad about it—that would have been an untenable thought for him. He figured they took it as philosophically as he did. And he meant no harm or cruelty toward them. He only commented on what to him was an accident of nature that no one could change.

At times, his treatment of people seems callous, but it wasn't so; he had a tremendous affection for people. It's just that he refused to overlook what seemed to him remarkable and amusing about them. This went for any aspect of a person's condition—his looks, his age, his status, his attitude—and almost everyone's particular circumstance was worthy of attention.

RUSH: (*Going*) Hey, wasn't that lady at Stembottom's funny tonight? I hadda laugh.

SADE: She's an invalid lady, son.

RUSH: What's the matter with her?

SADE: She's got nervousness. Now, go to bed. Don't stand there in the cold.

RUSH: Night.

SADE:	Good night.
RUSH:	Night, Gov.
VIC:	(*Who Has Been In A Doze*) Huh?
RUSH:	Good night.
VIC:	Good night. Seems to me this makes about the third time we've exchanged felicitations.
RUSH:	(*Laughing*) Ya mad?
VIC:	(*Grunt*)
RUSH:	(*Laughing*) I thought that lady was mad tonight. Kept slappin' herself.
SADE:	Go to bed, son, for goodness sake.
RUSH:	What'd that lady slap herself for?
SADE:	She was nervous.
RUSH:	What makes her nervous?
SADE:	You—go—to—bed.
RUSH:	(*Laughing*) Night, Mom.

Says McClaughery: "Paul always had the gift of seeing something funny in situations which others would view with indifference or solemnity. It used to make me mad that when we were on an elevated train or something, Paul and I would see exactly the same things, but he saw something funny. When he pointed the humor out to me, I saw it all right, but couldn't see it for myself, or before Paul pointed it out to me."

RUSH: Oh, look, here comes Harry Jamieson on his coal wagon.

VIC: Rush, I don't think the sight of Harry Jamieson on his coal wagon is enough to keep us from doin' our work.

RUSH: He looks so funny, though.

VIC: What's funny about Harry?

RUSH: I think a fella drivin' a coal wagon always looks funny wearin' a derby hat.

VIC: Harry wearin' his derby?

RUSH: Yeah. Look at 'im.

VIC: An' I was just about to take a shovelful of snow. Well, I guess . . . say (**Chuckles**) Harry does look strange, don't he?

RUSH: Uh-huh . . . in the summertime he wears a stockin' cap an' in the wintertime he wears a derby. Guess that's because he's in-sane.

VIC: Aw, Harry ain't really insane.

RUSH: Kinda in-sane, ain't he?

VIC: Just a touch, maybe.

Frank Walsh writes: "Over and over again in letters and postal cards Paul would say to his correspondent something like this: 'I believe I will go down to the Union Station and watch the folks check their luggage.' This always got the laugh it was supposed to from his auditors who couldn't imagine this urbane gent setting up an apparently mindless project. But the important point is: he did go down to the Union Station (or in later years he found more action at the bus station) to watch the folks come and go.

Sometimes it was embarrassing to be with Paul—at the racetrack or somewhere. If a person came along who was funny looking in some way, especially tall or short, popeyed or with thick glasses, or even crippled, Paul would snicker and poke me in the ribs and make some remark, usually in earshot of the subject. The remark was usually so outrageously tasteless I couldn't help breaking up no matter how I tried to control myself, but I'd be cringing at the same time and imploring him with my eyes to lower his voice. But Paul would just cackle away, and nudge me, looking straight at the person, and if they happened to turn and meet his eye they'd usually just give him a blank stare and pass on. What they'd see, of course, was a very distinguished looking guy, especially in later years, with his white hair and classic features. What they thought when they saw this dignified gentleman acting in such an outlandish way was probably that the poor fellow was not right in his head and so they continued on their way with their dignity intact and even feeling good about not paying any special notice. If a pregnant woman was going by, Paul might start to giggle, holding his hand over his mouth and pointing, pretending to be surreptitious, but of course being obvious as hell. The woman would smile sadly and continue to waddle on by.

At a party he might be the soul of propriety, but he also might decide to be devilish.

At a large New Year's Eve party thrown by Cliff Norton, Paul was sitting next to an old school chum of Cliff's, a mousey little guy, not in the business. As Cliff tells it: "I suppose poor Stanley was just trying to make a few pleasant remarks, and Paul suddenly leaped up and just screamed: 'Cliff! This man is making improper advances!'"

Or Paul, on meeting someone for the first time and listening to their polite chatter for a few moments, might say, very quietly and directly, "This is the most boring conversation I've ever had."

Once when he was introduced to some gorgeous movie star who was stopping in Chicago, he shook her hand, leaned over and whispered in her ear, "I've got a nineteen twenty-six Essex parked outside. Would you like to go somewhere and screw?" Of course,

Billy and Paul.

after the initial shock, most people laughed and I guess the movie star was no exception.

Talking to Paul, and reading his letters too, is sometimes like little electric shocks, or getting pelted with ice water. He shakes you with his frankess, his lucidity, his audaciousness. But the wonderful thing about him was that, with people he knew, he could make them enjoy their own amusing aspects as much as he did. He was also just as willing to laugh at anything ludicruous about himself. It was a quality that endeared him to people. They trusted him, trusted his affection and objectivity, saw there was nothing personal in his observation, no malice, no animosity and no cruelty. If this seems difficult to believe, I'm not surprised, but that's the way he was.

"Mr. Jorgerson of the 2nd Slovenian Reformed Church spoke to us young people at the 'Y' on Monday night. He lectured on Jacking Off, showing us many interesting slides of people Jacking Off. As soon as I finish this note I will start Jacking Off. You can't beat Jacking Off."

In 1933 Vic and Sade appeared at the World's Fair in Chicago and performed on closed circuit television, one of the new wonders of the age (and shades of doom to come). Paul used the visit as the basis of a script.

VIC:	Look at this guy comin'. Sade.
SADE:	Where?
VIC:	Walkin' along beside the water. With . . .
SADE:	(*Delighted*) Oh. Little midget. Son, look at the little midget.
RUSH:	Yeah.
SADE:	(*Delighted*) Ain't he tiny? Person just wouldn't believe he was a grown-up man. (*Lower Tones*) Say, maybe we hadn't better stare at him so. Might hurt his feelin's.
VIC:	He gets paid to be stared at.
SADE:	Yes, when he's puttin' on his stunts in the show. But when he's just walkin' around the World's Fair, I bet . . .
RUSH:	(*Calls*) Hi.
SADE:	(*Horrified*) Son.
RUSH:	(*Laughs*) He answered me, didn't he?

Vic:	That midget a friend of yours, son?
Rush:	I talked to him a little this morning.
Sade:	When was that?

Gran'pa Snyder was a character that began to appear in the shows. Gran'pa was an old duck in his eighties who lived with an unmarried daughter. Another daughter, married, who lived in town, shared the responsibility of him. He was loved by his daughters and all, but he was also something of a trial due to his advanced years and limited capacities.

One day Gran'pa's daughter asks Rush if he can take care of the old man for fifty cents that afternoon, and Rush would like to do it, except he has school. At noontime he comes home and broaches the problem to his folks. Sade says absolutely no, he can't cut school.

Rush:	Hey, how's this? I could take Gran'pa Snyder to school an' leave him in the boys' wash room.
Sade:	Lands, son.
Rush:	He'd like that. Guys goin' in an' out all day. Plenty of company. An' when kids get excused from class to go there, they kill all the time they can.
Sade:	Wouldn't be a very nice place to spend a whole afternoon.
Rush:	No-o. I guess Mis' Ruth and Mis' Helen Snyder'd ask me where we'd been an' I'd hafta tell.
Sade:	Of course.
Rush:	But I know Gran'pa Snyder'd like it O.K. Only drawback is . . .

SADE: Rush, I'm tired of watchin' you fiddle around with that plate. You jump in now an' eat your dinner.

RUSH: All right, but shucks, if there's any possible way to . . . Say, I got an idea. (*Gets Up*) Gonna make a telephone call.

SADE: (*To Vic*) Look at this nice potato with cheese all cold.

VIC: Nothing less than sacrilege.

RUSH: (*At Phone*) 9086-J, please. Correct. (*Aside*) If this works I'm all fixed. (*To Phone*) Hello . . . Mis' Skinner? This is Rush Meadows, Miss Skinner. Yes. Why . . . a . . . the reason I called up was . . . would there be any objection if I brought a visitor to class this afternoon? His name is Mr. Snyder. No, he isn't a little boy, he's an older gentleman. Yes. Quite an old gentleman. Yes. Why, he's . . . he's a friend. Yes. Would it be all right. Uh-huh. Thank you very much, Miss Skinner. Yes, ma'am. Yes, ma'am. Goodbye. (*Hangs Up*) (*To The Others, With Some Jubilance*) I get to take him to class.

SADE: (*Who Feels That There's Something Vaguely Wrong About This*) Well, is that all right? I mean are ya s'sposed to . . .

RUSH: Sure. Gran'pa Snyder'll sit beside my desk in his wheelchair an' be a visitor. Prob'ly have a swell time. He can listen to the kids recite an' talk all he wants during recess an' . . . an' just have a picnic.

VIC: Looks like your fifty cents is in the bag, Hank.

RUSH: Sure. Now I'll eat, Mom. Everything's off my chest.

SADE: Mighty good thing. Here's bread. Hop in. I'll heat up the gravy for your potato.

VIC: By the way, now that your troubles have resolved themselves into bright rainbows of joy, perhaps you'll solve the mystery of them two phone calls ya got.

RUSH: Glad to. Mis' Ruth Snyder called me the first time an' Mis' Helen Snyder called me up the second time.

SADE: What'd they want?

RUSH: Wanted to talk to their gran'pa.

SADE: What made 'em think he'd be here?

RUSH: Well . . . a . . . I didn't tell you this before, but I took that job when Mis' Snyder offered it to me.

SADE: Took it?

RUSH: Yeah . . . I . . . I brought Gran'pa Snyder here with me.

VIC & SADE: Home with ya?

RUSH: Uh-huh . . . I didn't want you to see him until I found out if you'd let me cut school so I . . .

VIC & SADE: Where is Gran'pa Snyder?

RUSH: Got him out in the woodshed.

VIC & SADE: Woodshed!

RUSH: Yeah, but don't worry. He's O.K. Sittin' in his wheelchair sleepin' like a baby. Pass me the salt an' pepper, Gov?

END OF SCRIPT.

My friend McClaughery is worried about approaching old age. He said he took a copy of the **Woman's Home Companion** into the crapper the other day with a view to playing with himself. He fastened his eyes on a voluptuous corset ad and started. After a while he was horrified to discover that he'd slackened speed and was reading the Household Hints.

Paul considered the lives of most people comical and ridiculous, especially, as he called them, "working stiffs." Vic's absorption in Kitchenware typified Paul's attitude toward the pursuits and livelihoods of most people.

"Chief Accountant of Consolidated Kitchenware, Plant Number Fourteen" was always said by Vic with an air of importance—a comment on the pride most people take in their pedestrian jobs.

Paul thought his own work was pretty insignificant too, in the larger scheme of things, and was often thoughtful about why anyone was willing to pay any of us so much money to do the rather silly thing we were doing. "It's because it's so highly specialized," he concluded finally. I don't know what he really considered important work, never found out. He admired some of the giants of literature, Tolstoy, Dickens, Shaw, O'Hara. Not much else. Guess he secretly wanted to be a great writer.

As the show progressed it became more and more a satire on small-town life, and life in general, although I'm sure a great portion of our listeners never saw it that way. In its hey-day, which lasted a good eight years or so, **Vic and Sade** was always at, or very close to, the top of the Crosley Ratings for daytime shows. But it appealed to listeners on several distinct levels. First, there were the average housewives who saw the show as a pleasant little slice of life in a small town. Second, there were the more perceptive civilians that realized a gentle bite was being taken here and there.

Then there were the people in show business who recognized the craft that went into the writing and execution of the show. We were always getting word of how such and such a famous movie star in Hollywood would stop work on the set so that everyone could listen to us. Walter Huston was one of our most avid fans.

Whenever he was in Chicago he would come and sit in the control room and watch us work. (At those times I usually did a very lousy performance.) And then finally, there was that elevated group of "observers" (like Paul) who saw the show as a specimen of folklore, of Americana. Who recognized Paul for what he was—one of the great humorists of his day. Hendrik VanLoon commented that Paul was doing some of the greatest folk writing of the time. James Thurber and John O'Hara took notice of the show in articles for the *New Yorker* and *Cosmopolitan*. James Gould Cozzens, Upton Sinclair, Gluyas Williams wrote fan letters.

Famous fans.

In script number forty-nine, Vic is going to write a book on Kitchenware. "The Ideals of Kitchenware." This book was commissioned by Mr. Ruebush. If it was any good it would be distributed to all the Consolidated Kitchenware people all over the country.

VIC: "The glorious part of the Kitchenware business inspires us to greater efforts on behalf of a still greater future . . . " No. "The Kitchenware business is built on a foundation as solid and enduring as the Rock of Gibral . . . " . . . "Kitchenware may be likened unto a little blue flower that . . . "

VIC: "Kitchenware reduced to its lowest terms is simply a manifestation of Man's resolve to better himself and his fellow . . ."

VIC: "When the infant, 'Kitchenware,' lay in his cradle and all over the world the first glimmering of progress began to . . ." (**Phone**)

The Kitchenware Dealer's Quarterly was the Bible of Vic's business. When it arrived at the house, everything stopped for Vic until he read it cover to cover. He also constantly deceived himself that it's contents might be as interesting to Sade and Rush as they were to him. Of course, the latter two could barely conceal their lack of interest which set up those cross currents of purpose that Paul loved to play with. He got a lot of mileage from the *Kitchenware Dealer's Quarterly,* so it arrived at the house at least a dozen times a year, which is pretty good for a Quarterly.

VIC: Sade, here's a little poem Ollie Goofer wrote. Wanta hear it?

RUSH: Hey, I'm tellin' about somethin'.

VIC: One side, please. Listen to this now. Name of the poem is "Ah, Kitchenware—Civilization's Precious Boon."

SADE: Ollie Goofer wrote it, huh?

VIC: Right out of his own head. Ollie's clever that way.

	Know where this magazine goes, dontcha?
SADE:	No.
VIC:	All over the United States. One copy goes to the White House. President Roosevelt's got a free subscription.
SADE:	Ya s'pose he reads it?
VIC:	'Course he reads it. He's got to know what's goin' on.
SADE:	S'pose he'll read Ollie's piece?
VIC:	Sure. It's on the very first page. He couldn't miss it.
SADE:	It's nice for Ollie, ain't it?
VIC:	Sure. Listen now. "Ah, Kitchenware—Civilization's Precious Boon." (*Swallows And Prepared To Read Emotionally*) Adam an' Eve were a jolly pair. They lived in the jungle I don't know where. They had no kitchenware at their disposal. That didn't come until several centures later.'
SADE:	That the first verse?
VIC:	Uh-huh. Here's the second: "On Noah's ark so 'tis said. They had no kitchenware in which to bake their bread. No pots an' pans were their . . .
RUSH:	Gov.
VIC:	Huh?
RUSH:	I got somethin' to show Mom.

VIC: Do you think it's polite to interrupt a fella when he's readin' aloud?

RUSH: No, but . . .

VIC: Very well then. Be seated. I mean be quiet.

SADE: He has got somethin' to show us, Vic.

VIC: I am to understand then that you don't care to hear any more of Ollie's poem?

SADE: (*To Rush*) Wait just a second, son. Let Gov finish the little piece.

VIC: Ya listenin'?

SADE: Uh-huh.

VIC: "On Noah's ark so 'tis said. They had no kitchenware in which to bake their bread. No pots an' pans for cooking had they. But kitchenware was destined to eventually come into existence."

SADE: Second verse, huh?

VIC: Yeah. This ain't such a good poem as I thought.

SADE: Don't rhyme.

RUSH: That's one trouble with it.

VIC: Well, here's the third verse. "Cleopatra was the Queen of the Nile. She used to the Roman generals beguile. She used a very primitive type of kitchenware, but during the following fifty years there were many improvements."

SADE: Is that all?

VIC: Yeah.

SADE: (*Non-Commital*) Um.

VIC: Not so hot, is it?

APRIL 22, 1964

My father-in-law is staying with us a few days. He was eighty years old on Monday and celebrated by going to Lake Michigan and getting a disabling case of sunburn. One morning last week he was on the way home from the grocery store. He thought he'd stop by the flat of an old pal who has recently changed addresses. His thought was to say, "Hello, Harry, nice place you've got here . . ." and go on. He stayed 16 hours. Every time it got to be meal time his buddy would say, "Murray, have lunch with me," or "Have breakfast with me," or "Have midnight snack with me." My father-in-law accepted all invitations. Very likely he didn't have many groceries left to take home. This makes me think of another story about him. He was invited by a bathing beach crony to a Polish party. He attended the party in this very neighborhood. This was the conduct of the evening: each guest was given a smoked eel and a funny paper. There were army cots all over the apartment. You lay down on an army cot, ate your smoked eel, and read your funny paper. There was no booze. When you'd finished your smoked eel and were all through laughing at Mutt and Jeff you got up off your army cot, turned off the dangling electric light and tiptoed home.

Chapter Six — 1933

ANNOUNCER: It is evening as our scene opens now, and here in the living room under the red glow of the floor lamp we discover two gentlemen deep in a game of checkers. The gentlemen are Victor Gook and his young son, Rush . . . and young son Rush is saying . . .

RUSH: Your move, Gov.

VIC: Give a man time.

RUSH: You only got one more move.

VIC: That's what you say.

RUSH: Well, that's right.

VIC: You don't know to what lengths of strategy I may resort to.

RUSH: I don't know what?

VIC: Nothin'.

RUSH: I don't know nothin'?

VIC: No.

RUSH: (*Laughs*) Aw, g'wan an' move that checker, Gov. It's the only one you can move an' soon as you move it you're beat.

VIC: A man is never beat till he says he is.

RUSH: Well, you're beat. Soon as you move that checker.

VIC: Suppose I decline to move that checker?

RUSH: Ya hafta move that checker.

VIC: Son, did you ever hear of the Roman General Arcengetorix?

RUSH: No.

VIC: I'd like to tell you a little story about the Roman General Arcengetorix.

RUSH: (*Laughs*) Aw, Gov, c'mon an' move the checker. Then we'll start another game.

VIC: You don't care to hear the story about the Roman General Arcengetorix?

RUSH: Sure, but I'd like to—

VIC: Hey, whatcha doin'?

RUSH: Movin' your checker for ya.

VIC: Hands off that checker.

RUSH: It's the only one you can move.

VIC: Let that checker alone. My story about the Roman

	General Arcengetorix has a strong bearing on that checker.
RUSH:	Yeah, but I'd like to get the game over with an' start another.
VIC:	Please compose yourself to listen to this story.
RUSH:	All right.
VIC:	Very well. The Roman General Arcengetorix was captured by the Carthaginians.
RUSH:	Who?
VIC:	The Carthaginians.
RUSH:	Who are they?
VIC:	It is not essential to your comprehension of the story that you know who the Carthaginians were. Suffice it to say they were the enemies of the Roman General Arcengetorix.
RUSH:	I don't even know who he is.
VIC:	It is not important that you do.
RUSH:	How'm I gonna understand the story unless you tell me who . . .
VIC:	Listen an' you'll understand. The Roman General Arcengetorix was captured by the Carthaginians after a bloody battle of nine days duration. Just as they were about to put him to death, their general stepped forth an' said to Arcengetorix, "Is there any requet you'd like to make before you die?"

Arcengetorix said, "Yes. I'd like a cup of water." "Very well," said the General, "here it is," and he handed him a cup of water. "Arcengetorix," said the General, "I promise no harm will befall you till you've drunk that cup of water." Well, sir, ya know what Arcengetorix done?

RUSH: What'd he do?

VIC: He threw that cup on the ground hard as he could an' broke it in a thousand pieces.

RUSH: (*Impressed*) Huh!

VIC: So the Carthaginians had to let him go. Ya see they promised they wouldn't hurt him till he drank that water.

RUSH: An' he couldn't drink it, huh?

VIC: 'Course not. It was all over the ground.

RUSH: (*Impressed*) Huh!

VIC: Pretty good story, ain't it?

RUSH: Sure is.

VIC: Now maybe you won't bellyache so much about me movin' that checker.

RUSH: (*In The Dark*) No-o.

VIC: Shall we start another game?

RUSH: This one ain't over with yet.

VIC: I am giving you this game.

RUSH: You don't hafta give it to me. Move your checker an' I'll win the game.

VIC: Rush, have you forgotten Arcengetorix so soon?

RUSH: No-o, but . . .

VIC: Very well, then.

RUSH: Pickin' up the checkers?

VIC: Yeah, didn't you say you wished to play another game?

RUSH: Yeah.

VIC: That's what I thought. Which do you want—the red ones or the black ones?

RUSH: Red ones.

VIC: Good. I'll take the black ones.

RUSH: Gov, I won that game, didn't I?

VIC: I gave you that game.

RUSH: But, Gov, if you'd taken your move I'd won.

VIC: No man can say about that.

RUSH: But I would of, Gov. You only had one move. If you'd taken it, I'd a . . .

VIC: (*A Little Sadly*) I guess the story of Arcengetorix meant very little to you.

RUSH: No, but . . . (*Pause*)

VIC: But what?

RUSH: Nothin', I guess.

VIC: Very well, then. It's your move.

RUSH: I get credit for that last game, don't I?

VIC: Sure. What made you think you didn't?

RUSH: Well, I dunno, I . . . all right. I'll move here.

VIC: I'll move here.

RUSH: I'll move here.

VIC: I'll move here.

RUSH: This is the championship game you know, Gov.

VIC: Is it?

RUSH: Yeah. You won the first one, an' I won the second. This one is for the championship.

VIC: Uh-huh. I'll move here.

RUSH: I'll move here.

VIC: I'll jump ya.

RUSH: I'll jump ya back.

VIC: Very good.

❖ ❖ ❖ ❖

At this point, Sade enters with a problem to solve and, after some pages, it is disposed of. Then Vic and Rush turn their attention back to the checker game:

RUSH: Gov.

VIC: Yeah?

RUSH: If I get ya where ya only got one move left like I done the last game, will ya take the move?

VIC: Of course.

RUSH: Ya won't tell me about some Roman General an' then give me the game, will ya?

VIC: There will be no necessity for that.

RUSH: I'd kinda like to play the game out.

VIC: O.K. Where ya gonna move?

RUSH: I'll move here.

VIC: I'll move here.

RUSH: I'll move here.

END OF SCRIPT

ANNOUNCER: Which concludes for today our little interlude with Vic, Sade and Rush.

COMMERCIAL CREDIT

R.T. McClaughery is looking for a young beautiful and passionate woman who is interested in enjoying sex at the conversation level.

September 15 in the world of Vic and Sade dawned unseasonable cold. Sade is downstairs preparing breakfast, while upstairs Vic and Rush are sleepily putting on their clothes:

VIC: (*Up*) Why don't you put on your pants?

RUSH: Too cold.

VIC: A very peculiar way to figure. It seems to me like a fella would only run around without his pants in cases where it's too hot.

RUSH: Mom'll prob'ly have it warm in the kitchen. When there's a stove ya get warmer without your pants than with 'em.

VIC: Well, c'mon.

RUSH: I'm ready.

VIC: Doggone, it's getting' cold. Listen to that wind howl outside.

RUSH: Soon be winter-time, won't it?

VIC: Just a couple months now.

SADE: (*Calling*) You gentlemen comin'?

VIC & RUSH: (*Answering*) Yeah.

SADE: Well, hurry.

VIC: It occurs to me that the morale of this household is slipping when members of the family are permitted to go to breakfast without their pants.

RUSH: I'll put 'em on as soon as we get in the kitchen where it's warm.

VIC: What leads you to believe it's gonna be warm in the kitchen?

RUSH: Mom'll have the oven door open. She sure can make it warm with just a gas stove.

VIC: Um.

RUSH: Mom's a very smart lady.

VIC: She's just smart enough to lay down the law about you not wearin' pants. Do you think President Roosevelt ever went to breakfast without his pants?

RUSH: I don't know.

VIC: He did not. All through life President Roosevelt made it his motto to always wear pants at social functions, not excluding breakfast. Look where President Roosevelt is today. His simple motto carries him to the peak of . . .

SADE: (*Cheerily*) Good morning, gentlemen.

VIC & RUSH: Morning

❖ ❖ ❖ ❖

Fart Williams:

As a matter of fact I haven't been at all remiss in my epistolary obligations to you. For six months I wrote you a long letter every day. In each letter I enclosed a $100 bank note. On Friday the Post Office Department returned me all that mail in a large business envelope. It seemed I had been careless. The letters were all addressed to:

> Mr. Willis Idelman
> 4884 White Rock
> Anselmo, Colorado

I expect that little slip on my part coaxes a chuckle from you as it does from me. My first thought was to air mail you the parcel without delay but I needed the $18,000 the letters contained so I'll postpone the whole thing until August 22. Better write that down on your calendar. You might not want $18,000 in your house over night and this notice will enable you to make plans.

VIC AND SADE   (*John F. Jelke Company*)

11:00 TO 11:14 A.M. C.D.S.T.   SEPTEMBER 21, 1933   THURSDAY

INTRODUCTION: Our scene opens in the living room now, and here's Vic at the library table, all manner of important looking documents spread out before him. We gather that he's working at home today. And who's this coming in from the kitchen. It's Sade, looking sweet and clean in her cap and apron, and carrying a broom. She surveys her industrious husband a moment and says . . .

SADE: Vic.

VIC: Yeah?

SADE: You haven't started workin' yet, have you?

VIC: Yeah.

SADE: Not writin'.

VIC: No, but my mind is achurn with what I'm gonna write.

SADE: Wish you'd take a minute off to help me.

VIC: I hafta get at these invoices, Sade. That's why I'm home . . . so I can work in peace and quiet.

SADE: This won't take but five minutes.

VIC: I'm workin'.

SADE: You're not writin' anything. Just sittin' there.

VIC: I'd like to point out to you, Mrs. Gook, that three fourths of the world's work is done by fellas who are "just sittin' there." Edison was "just sittin' there" when he invented the incandescent lamp. President Washington was "just sittin' there" when the immortal words of the Gettysburg Address went through his head. Napoleon was "just sittin' there" when he won the battle of Waterloo, Benjamin Franklin was . . .

A man who believed in coming directly to the point met a beautiful woman and said: "Happy to form your acquaintance. I'd like a little pussy." She answered: "So would I. Mine is as big as a catcher's mitt."

GEORGE: What were you doing in that sidewalk café last night?
WILLIS: That wasn't any sidewalk café, that was my furniture.

SEPTEMBER 21, 1933

VIC: (*In Paper*) Sade.

SADE: Yes.

VIC: Ella Wheeler's leg is knitting nicely.

SADE: (*Startled*) Her leg is?

VIC: She broke it.

SADE: Yes, I know but . . . (*Giggles*) Oh, I see. When you said her leg was knitting, her bein' a dress-maker an' all, I thought for a minute . . . (*Giggles*) What else does it say?

VIC: That's all.

SADE: The paper just states her leg is knitting?

VIC: Nicely.

SADE: What?

VIC: Nicely. Her leg is knitting nicely.

SADE: Well read to me what the paper states.

VIC: (*Reads*) Mrs. R.K. Wheeler of 1912 West Market Street, reports that the leg of her daughter, who is vacationing at home from a year in Chicago, is knitting nicely.

SADE: Does the paper really state that?

VIC: I just read it to ya.

SADE: What a funny way to say it. Sounds like it's her leg that's vacationing in Chicago.

VIC: (*Chuckles*) Uh-huh. Does at that.

SADE: That paper comes out with the strangest things. Worded so funny, ya know. Remember when Mis' Pitchmeyer broke her leg?

VIC:	Bath-tub, wasn't it?
SADE:	Yes, but did you read what the paper stated?
VIC:	Don't remember.
SADE:	Well, it told about her slippin' in the bath-tub an' all, but it referred to her leg as a "member."
VIC:	Member, huh?
SADE:	Yes. Member this an' member that. The member was broke in two places. The member will have to be put in a plaster cast. The member has been givin' severe pain. Mis' Pitchmeyer was pretty much put out about it. Called up the head fella at the newspaper an' everything.
VIC:	(*Chuckles*) Shucks.
SADE:	I guess them newspaper fellas are pretty much smart alecks.

❖ ❖ ❖ ❖

Last week I changed my name to Schul Greenspan and this week they passed a law that no Jewish guy is allowed within 20 miles of the Desplaines River so I have moved to Bucyrus, Ohio. I advise you to change your name to Mildred McDermott.

NOVEMBER 11, 1933

RUSH:	(*Laughs*) Hey, talkin' about bein' hungry makes me think of what Walt Keefer told me about his uncle.
SADE:	Don't stop workin'.
RUSH:	Walt said that his uncle that lives in Carlinsville

	had his throat shot in the war, so he can't eat.
SADE:	My lands. Stamp that down good, Vic.
VIC:	Um.
RUSH:	Ya know how he eats?
SADE:	Who? Oh—Walter's uncle?
RUSH:	Yes. Nothin'll go down his throat, see, so the doctor fixed a tube from his stomach up to his coat pocket.
SADE:	(*In Disbelief*) Heavens.
RUSH:	That's what Walt said. So when his uncle goes in a restaurant or somewhere an' gets somethin' to eat, he just takes it an' puts it in his pocket. (*Laughs*)
SADE:	(*Laughs*) I don't believe it.
RUSH:	Sounds awful fishy, don't it?
SADE:	Lands, yes.
RUSH:	Walt said he went in a cafeteria one time an' his uncle ordered coffee, an' when they brought the coffee, Walt's uncle took it an' poured it in his pocket.
SADE:	(*Laughs*) Aw.
RUSH:	(*Laughs*) That's right. An' then he poured in some cream an' sugar.

Throughout the life of the show, Sade got countless letters from her sister Bess. Bess and Walter became familiar and distinctive characters even though they never even came for a visit. Their personalities developed strictly through the correspondence between Sade and Bess, and many a show revolved around the attitudes of our characters toward Bess' letters. Vic and Rush were inclined to treat the letters with cautious derision; Sade was defensive about her sister and brother-in-law. On November 11, 1933 (I'm pretty sure), Sade received her first letter from Bess.

SADE: (*Reads*) I don't know whether you remember that Mrs. Frawley two houses from us or not. Anyway, she passed forward late Tuesday night. I never knew her very well, but . . . (*To Vic*) That mean she died?

VIC: What?

SADE: Says she passed forward.

VIC: Sure.

SADE: She died?

VIC: I s'pose.

SADE: Well, dontcha say "passed on"?

VIC: Read the rest.

SADE: Anyway she passed forward late Tuesday night. I never knew her very well, but I know she was a nice lady. The funeral was yesterday. Walt an' I went. There were just oceans of flowers an' . . . (*Aside*) Yeah, she died.

❖ ❖ ❖ ❖

THURSDAY, NOVEMBER 9

RUSH: Every move I make playin' checkers you say is

	a stupid move.
VIC:	I never like to obscure the truth. I have moved.
RUSH:	(*Laughs*) Very stupid move.
VIC:	I say nothing. However, I am thinking with some satisfaction that I recently won the championship of the Universe. Suppose you move.
RUSH:	Yeah. I'll move here.
VIC:	Uh-huh.
RUSH:	Gov, how big is the Universe?
VIC:	Eight by eleven.
RUSH:	Eight by eleven what?
VIC:	I don't remember the details.

❖ ❖ ❖ ❖

SADE:	(*Giggling*) Look, Vic.
VIC:	Baby clothes.
SADE:	Uh-huh . . . for Mac an' Dorothy. Ya see it'll be about Christmas time when . . . (*Giggles*) Ain't they cute? See, Rush?
RUSH:	Who's the baby pants for?
SADE:	They're for . . . Oh, a little baby.
RUSH:	What baby?

SADE: (*Giggles*) Never mind. Look here now. Whatcha think of this for Uncle Walt?

RUSH: Mom, you said Mac an' Dorothy, didn't ya?

SADE: I don't remember. Look what I got for Uncle Walt.

RUSH: Mac an' Dorothy ain't got any baby.

SADE: Look what I got for Uncle Walt.

VIC: Rush, look what Mom's got for Uncle Walt.

SADE: Just kind of a novelty is all. Uncle Walt don't expect much for Christmas. I'm goin' to send real nice things to the kids. Get away from there, Rush.

RUSH: Wanta see the baby stuff.

SADE: Never mind the baby stuff.

RUSH: What baby is it for?

SADE: Oh, it's . . . get away. Now look here.

❖ ❖ ❖ ❖

VIC: Yeah, Whose move is it?

RUSH: A . . . mine.

VIC: Move then.

RUSH: I'll move here.

VIC: Uh-huh.

RUSH:	That the one you wanta move?
VIC:	My having moved it is ample answer to your question.
RUSH:	I'll move . . . say, Gov.
VIC:	Huh?
RUSH:	Whose baby gets the baby clothes?
VIC:	I dunno.
RUSH:	Aw, ya do too. Mom said . . .
VIC:	Ya gonna play checkers? I've moved.
RUSH:	I'll move here.
VIC:	Very stupid move.

END OF SCRIPT

ANNOUNCER:	And so to supper. And so back to the living room. And so to bed. (*Pause*) (COMMERCIAL CREDIT)

DECEMBER 12, 1933

RUSH:	Mom.
SADE:	Yes?
RUSH:	May I be permitted to say a word?
SADE:	What?
RUSH:	I done something nice for you at school today.

SADE:	What was that?
RUSH:	You know what you said last night about Uncle Fletcher?
SADE:	About the letter you mean?
RUSH:	Yeah. You said it'd be nice if me and you and Gov wrote to him as much as we could an' cheer him up.
SADE:	Did you write to him?
RUSH:	We all did.
SADE:	Who all did?
RUSH:	Everybody in my room.
SADE:	All the children wrote letters to Uncle Fletcher?
RUSH:	Yeah. We're havin' letter-writin' an' I told the teacher about Uncle Fletcher bein' sick, an' she said we might just as well write to him.
SADE:	No.
RUSH:	I got all the letters right here in my pocket (*Reaches For Them*) There's thirty-six of 'em altogether. I bet Uncle Fletcher'll be so happy he . . .
VIC:	Hey. What's this letter say? Can't read it.
RUSH:	Hand it to me. (*Pause*) Gov, this letter is from Paul Keefer. He can't write very well because he's got a broken arm.
VIC:	I couldn't make head or tail to that letter.

RUSH: I can read it. Says "Dear Uncle Fletcher. I am a boy twelve years old. My arm is broke. Yours respectfully, Paul Keefer."

VIC: A very newsy letter. Oughta cheer Uncle Fletcher right up.

SADE: Rush, are you writin' a letter yourself to explain all these letters?

RUSH: Uh-uh. I figure thirty-six letters is enough to cheer anybody up.

VIC: He'll wonder who all these people are that wrote to him.

RUSH: They all got their names signed.

VIC: Yeah, but he'll wonder what the thunder. Suppose you got thirty-six letters from guys you never heard of?

RUSH: I'd be cheered up.

VIC: (*Laughs*) Shucks.

❖ ❖ ❖ ❖

VIC: Listen: "Dear Uncle Fletcher. Your bill is three weeks over-due. Kindly send us a check immediately or we shall be forced to get in touch with the authorities. Your friend, Mary Rogers."

RUSH: That's a business letter.

VIC: I'll say it is.

RUSH: Mary Rogers wrote it.

VIC: Uh-huh, oughta cheer Uncle Fletcher right up. Here's another. "Dear Uncle Fletcher, forgive me for what happened Tuesday. I didn't mean to hurt you. Mother forced me into marrying George. Can you meet me tonight? Your roses were lovely. Henrietta Price."

RUSH: That's a romantic letter.

VIC: Uh-huh.

RUSH: Henrietta Price wrote it.

VIC: It oughta brighten up Uncle Fletcher's sick bed.

SADE: Son, maybe you ought to write explainin' to Uncle Fletcher who these letters are from.

RUSH: Aw, no, Mom. Thirty-six letters is enough.

SADE: Well, suit yourself. C'mon, an' I'll fix you something to eat.

VIC: Just a second. Listen to this: "Dear Uncle Fletcher. The cemetery is beautiful now. All the graves are under a blanket of soft snow. Wish you were here. Charles Sweeting."

RUSH: That's a letter on a subject of general interest.

VIC: Uncle Fletcher's cheeriness will know no bounds.

RUSH: Charley Sweeting wrote it.

VIC: Here's one from Georgiana White.

RUSH: Georgiana White wrote an emotional letter.

VIC: I'll say she did.

RUSH: We hafta write all kinds of letters at school. I hadda write a letter of sympathy to . . .

SADE: C'mon, son.

VIC: Listen to this, Sade.

SADE: I wanta get this boy something to eat.

VIC: Listen to this: "Dear Uncle Fletcher. You were lovely last evening. Your cheeks were like wild-flowers in the moonlight. And your eyes:—like twin violets. Oh, Uncle Fletcher, will you listen to what is in my heart? If you could see my pillow wet with tears I know you'd fly to my side an' take me in your arms. You'll never see me again, Uncle Fletcher. Tonight I die. Georgiana White."

SADE: C'mon, son. I'll have the round steak hot in no time.

ANNOUNCER: Which concludes our little interlude with Vic, Sade and young Rush.

Paul observed the holidays, all of them. They provided ideas for scripts. But his special favorite was Christmas. There seemed no end of angles he could exploit concerning this important holiday. And you could trust Paul to stay on the dirt roads, off the main highways . . .

DECEMBER 19, 1933

SADE: Well—(*Reads*) Margaret and Steve were over for a little while Sunday. Margaret said she saw Cliff Waters in Freeport a week or so ago. He looks just the same as he always did. He's married now and they live in Sioux City Iowa. Now, Sade, I have something to ask you. Carson an' I had an argument about what size shoe Vic takes: ten and a half or eleven. Can you write an' tell us which is right. Maybe we're both wrong. Don't forget to do this now as we had quite an argument.

VIC: Aw, for Pete's sake. What a doggone thing to have an argument about.

SADE: (*Giggles*) Don't you catch on to that, Vic?

VIC: Catch on to what?

SADE: Don't you see why Pauline wants to know what size shoes you wear?

VIC: No.

SADE: (*Giggles*) I do.

VIC: What does she care what size shoe I wear?

SADE: I know why.

VIC: Why?

SADE: She wants to send you some shoes for Christmas.

VIC: Oh.

SADE: Sure. Maybe she's even makin' you some nice shoes. Bed-room slippers

VIC: Fine.

SADE: I better write first thing in the morning. What size do you wear?

VIC: Leven.

SADE: Leven, huh? Say, ain't that nice of her though?

VIC: Sure.

SADE: I was just wondering. Maybe it'd be better if you took your foot and . . .

VIC: If I took my foot?

SADE: Let me finish, why dontcha? I was gonna say maybe it'd be better if ya took your foot an' outlined it on a piece of paper. Then she'd be sure to get the right size. How'd that be?

VIC: O.K.

SADE: Good idea, don't ya think?

VIC: Fine. How'd it be to send her a shoe?

SADE: One of your shoes ya mean?

VIC: Sure.

SADE: No, I wouldn't do that. Be the same as hintin'.

Chapter Seven — 1934

In 1934 radio was really swinging into its golden years. The headliners were Al Pearce and His Gang, Burns and Allen, Eddie Cantor with Rubinoff and his violin, Ed Wynn, Fred Allen, George Jessel, Jack Benny, Jack Pearl, Joe Penner, Olson and Johnson, Phil Baker, Stoopnagle and Bud, Walter O'Keefe, Wheeler and Woolsey and Will Rogers. This is the year the National Barn Dance began, also Ted Weems. The "Carefree Carnival" was sponsored by Crazy Water and "The Ex-Lax Big Show" was sponsored, of course, by Ex-Lax. Castoria presented "The Castoria Program" with Tibault; yes—things were really moving. I.J. Fox sponsored "The Fur Trappers' Orchestra," and Old Gold had Fred Waring. Wonder Bread sponsored "The Happy Wonder Bakeries." There was "The Princess Pat Show" with the Morin Sisters. Yeast Foam sponsored "The Yeast Foamers" with Jan Garber's Orchestra; Tasty Yeast sponsored Baby Rose Marie. Pepto-Mangan sponsored the Playboy Trio; Feenamint had The Three X Sisters. Brillo presented Tito Guizar. Campana Italian Balm, "The First Nighter." This is the year "One Man's Family" began, sponsored by Kentucky Winner. And Socony Oil sponsored the "Socony-Land Sketches." Pacific Borax sponsored "Death Valley Days," and Eno Salts presented "Eno Crime Clues" (in two 30 minute installments), Ken-L Ration presented "The Rin-Tin-Tin Thriller," Pepsodent presented "The Goldbergs." Jad Salts sponsored "Easy Aces." General Mills presented "Jack Armstrong" and Ovaltine continued to give us "Little Orphan Annie." Ralson gave us "Tom Mix."

1934 was also a big year for Vic and Sade. We picked up another sponsor, Ironized Yeast, on March 26th and lost them by the middle of May. BUT—on November 5th, we did our first show for Crisco (Proctor and Gamble) who remained our sponsor for ten long years. During this time we were always number one or two in the daytime ratings, switching first places with Ma Perkins.

1934 was also a year in which Paul did some incredible writing. He really came into his own. Paul always wrote in streaks. He would write average shows for a while, then round into form and do a bunch of terrific ones. Well, in 1934 he was hot practically all year. Each day was a little gem. This was the year that really established him—to himself as well as the rest of the radio world. It's been said that radio produced no great writers, except for Paul Rhymer.

VIC AND SADE   FEBRUARY 13, 1934   TUESDAY

RUSH:	Mom, ya know what tapioca is?
SADE:	Why, sure.
RUSH:	What is it?
SADE:	Why it's a . . . lands, I guess I don't. (*Giggles*) Ain't that funny? Been eatin' it all my life. What is it?
RUSH:	You know what it is, Gov?
VIC:	Tapioca?
RUSH:	Yeah. What's the definition?
VIC:	Tapioca is the residue left in the churn-pots after the manufacture of boots an' shoes. It is cooled to 32 degrees Fahrenheit, placed in egg-shaped vessels an' allowed to ferment. After aging three years, it is cut into capsules the size of an egg an' . . .

❖   ❖   ❖   ❖

They say if you hold a red-hot poker up against your balls, it'll disguise your handwriting.

After all the scripts we did—more than 3,000 of them—there were four or five that Van, Bern and I agreed were the most memorable of all. One of them follows. I won't even tell you what it's about, so you can enjoy it as it comes:

VIC AND SADE   (*Ironized Yeast Company*)   PAUL RHYMER

BREAKING IN PIPE   10:15–10:30 P.M.   MAY 14, 1934   MONDAY

ANNOUNCER: Come with us, again, if you please, to the little house half-way up in the next block—where Vic and Sade live.

COMMERCIAL CREDIT

ANNOUNCER: It is late afternoon as we enter the little house on Virginia Avenue now, and our scene, strangely enough, opens in the basement. A gentleman of our acquaintance Mr. Victor Gook—is to be seen sitting on a chair with his feet against the furnace—and another gentleman of our acquaintance—Mr. Rush Meadows, just arrived from upstairs—surveys his father, and remarks . . .

RUSH: Hi, Gov.

VIC: Heigh ho.

RUSH: Mom said you were down here.

VIC: My corporeal presence is living testimony that Mom told the truth.

RUSH: Huh?

VIC: I am down here.

RUSH: Yeah. Mom said you were down here breaking in a new pipe for Mr. Ruebush.

VIC: Mom's reputation for veracity remains unsmirched.

RUSH: Is that the pipe in the package?

VIC: It is.

RUSH: Smoking tobacco in the other package?

VIC: Yes.

RUSH: Gonna smoke up, huh?

VIC: You've put your finger on my plans.

RUSH: Mind if I stick around an' watch you?

VIC: Not at all.

RUSH: Mom wouldn't let you smoke your pipe upstairs, huh?

VIC: It was deemed best that I come down to the cellar. Pipe smoke lingers in curtains an' leaves odors offensive to delicate nostrils. Don't spill any of that now. That's expensive tobacco.

RUSH: It's . . . (*Reads*) 'South Dakota Mine Run Fine Cut.'

VIC: Uh-huh—a brand the boss has smoked for thirty years.

RUSH: Picture of a lady kissin' a fella on the front.

VIC: Uh-huh.

RUSH: Funny lookin' lady.

VIC: She's supposed to be Nicotina, the Goddess of the Tobacco Harvest.

RUSH: What's the fella?

VIC: He's just a fella. The picture is somewhat allegorical. Represents a pipe-smoker tasting the joys of tobacco.

RUSH: Oh.

❖ ❖ ❖ ❖

RUSH: Whatcha doin' now, Gov?

VIC: Tamping the tobacco delicately down in the bowl. Watch closely in order to know the procedure when you get to be twenty-one. It's something of an art.

RUSH: You're just pokin' it down good an' tight.

VIC: So it appears to the naked eye. Really my sensitive finger tips are distributing the tobacco leaves in a counter-clock direction, so that each dainty morsel will yield its full fragrance.

RUSH: (*Laughs*) Shucks.

VIC: Wanta watch me light this?

RUSH: I'm watchin'.

VIC: First I draw the match briskly across a resisting surface. (*Strikes Match*) See?

RUSH: I know how to light a match.

VIC: Does no harm to learn these things thoroughly. Now I apply the flame to the bowl of the pipe. (*Puff*) I puff. (*Puffs*) I puff again. (*Puffs*) I puff some more.

RUSH: You got it lit now.

VIC: (*Puffing*) Yes, indeed.

RUSH: Is it good?

VIC: Highly enjoyable. How does it smell?

RUSH: All right.

VIC: (*Puffing*) Has a fine full-bodied bouquet, don't ya think?

RUSH: Has a what?

VIC: Smells good.

RUSH: Oh, yeah.

❖ ❖ ❖ ❖

RUSH: (*Admiringly*) You're sure smokin' up.

VIC: (*Smugly*) Thank you.

RUSH: Keep on smokin' that fast an' you'll soon have to fill up your good ol' pipe again.

VIC: Yes, indeed.

RUSH: (*Laughing*) I don't blame Mom for not lettin' you smoke upstairs. You smoke so darn fast.

❖ ❖ ❖ ❖

RUSH: You're not smokin' up so much now, Gov.

VIC: No.

RUSH: 'Bout out of tobacco?

VIC: I believe I still got a few whiffs left.

RUSH: Why dontcha fill up your good ol' pipe again?

VIC: That might be a good idea. Pretty strong down near the bottom.

RUSH: Gee, you sure smoked up, Gov. Look at all the clouds up there.

VIC: Yeah. Say, son.

RUSH: Yeah.

VIC: I think maybe I'll lay my pipe aside for a while. No use runnin' it in the ground.

RUSH: You haven't got it broke in yet.

VIC: No, but . . . I'm afraid I'll crack the bowl firin' the dickens out of it like this.

RUSH: We got all this tobacco.

VIC: Yes, I know, but . . . Fact of the matter is, I seem to remember that a pipe should be broke in gradually. A pipe is like a fine horse. You whip it an' abuse it an' what you got? You got . . .

RUSH: Aw, Gov. You said you'd smoke.

VIC: (*Resigned*) Give me the tobacco.

RUSH: Here. All open an' handy.

VIC: Stuffy down here, dontcha think?

RUSH: All that smoke.

VIC: Yeah.

RUSH: It's got fine full-bodied bouquet, though.

VIC: (*Gloomily*) Uh-huh.

❖ ❖ ❖ ❖

VIC: This is enough.

RUSH: You filled it up full the other time.

VIC: (*Uneasily*) Did I?

RUSH: Yeah. Fill up your good ol' pipe.

VIC: Where's the tobacco?

RUSH: Right there in your lap.

VIC: Oh

RUSH: Why dontcha smoke up?

VIC: I . . . I guess I'm outa matches.

RUSH: (*Promptly*) Here's one.

VIC:	(*Sluggishly*) Thank you.
RUSH:	Ain't you gonna light it?
VIC:	Sure.
RUSH:	(*Cheerfully*) You don't need to be afraid if it goes out. I got plenty more.
VIC:	Yeah.
RUSH:	You didn't tamp the tobacco down this time.
VIC:	A . . . you wanta do it?
RUSH:	Sure.
VIC:	Here.
RUSH:	I might be a little slow doin' it. Never done it before.
VIC:	Take plenty of time. Take all the time you need.
RUSH:	(*Giggles*) I guess I've won your confidence, Gov.
VIC:	(*Sluggishly*) Huh?
RUSH:	I guess I've won your confidence. Little while ago you wouldn't let me touch your pipe.
VIC:	No. I mean yes.
RUSH:	You mean no.
VIC:	I mean no?
RUSH:	Yes.

VIC:		Um. (*Expels What Amounts To A Belch*)
RUSH:		Whatcha say?
VIC:		Nothin'.
RUSH:		I was gonna tell you about Sir Walter Raleigh. Well, he saw the Indians smokin' so he decided he'd smoke himself. So when he got back to Germany, he . . .
VIC:		(*Gloomily*) Where?
RUSH:		Germany. Sir Albert Raleigh lived in Germany.
VIC:		Who?
RUSH:		Sir Albert Raleigh. He lived in Germany.
VIC:		Oh. What time is it?
RUSH:		I don't know.
VIC:		Go upstairs and find out, will ya?
RUSH:		I think it's about quarter to five.
VIC:		Five?
RUSH:		Yeah. Wait. Mom's alarm clock's sitting' on the wash machine. Lean back an' you can see it.
VIC:		You lean back.
RUSH:		I'd hafta get up to see the alarm clock.
VIC:		You lean back.

RUSH:	What's the matter, Gov?
VIC:	(*Parroting Him*) What's the matter?
RUSH:	Dontcha feel good?
VIC:	Who me? Feel good?
RUSH:	Yeah.
VIC:	I feel good. What time is it?
RUSH:	I'll look and see.
VIC:	Find out what time it is.
RUSH:	(*Getting Up*) It's a . . .
VIC:	Go upstairs an' ask Mom what time is it.
RUSH:	The alarm clock's right here.
VIC:	What time is it?
RUSH:	It's a . . . twenty minutes to five.
VIC:	Go upstairs an' see what time is it?
RUSH:	It's twenty minutes to five, I said.
VIC:	Thanks.
RUSH:	Now you can smoke up.
VIC:	Thanks.
RUSH:	Gov, what's the matter?

VIC: Matter?

RUSH: Yeah. You look like . . . Hey, Gov. Gov. (*Calls*) Hey, Mom, can you come down here a minute? Hurry up!

END OF SCRIPT

ANNOUNCER: . . . which concludes tonight's brief interlude with the folks who live half-way up in the next block.

COMMERCIAL CREDIT

On the back of this script were some figures in Paul's handwriting. There are figures like this on a great many of his scripts. What he was figuring I don't know.

NOVEMBER 13, 1934

SADE: Mis' Gregg stopped in a minute this morning.

VIC: How's Cal?

SADE: Better. He recognizes his food.

VIC: Recognizes it?

SADE: Yes. You know how he was there for a while. Didn't know anybody?

VIC: Does he know anybody now?

SADE: No-o—don't know any people.

VIC: Just knows his food, huh?

SADE: Yes. Eats it right down. Uses a knife an' fork as frisky as a colt.

❖ ❖ ❖ ❖

SADE WANTS TO EVICT MR. POWERS FROM SHED   (*Crisco*)

NOVEMBER 16, 1934   FRIDAY

ANNOUNCER: Once again we present your friends Vic and Sade—at whose small house half-way up in the next block you are invited to spend a little while at this time.

COMMERCIAL CREDIT

ANNOUNCER: It is late afternoon as our scene opens now, and here in the living room we discover a man and his young son matching wits in a game of rummy. The card players are Vic and Rush . . . and since a hotly contested hand has just been concluded, it might be a good time for us to step up close . . . and listen.

RUSH: I win, Gov.

VIC: So you do.

RUSH: You lose.

VIC: A natural sequence—since you win.

RUSH: Know what the loser is, don'tcha?

VIC: It escapes me for the moment.

RUSH: An ol' dirty banana peel with all the insides scooped out.

VIC: Ah, yes.

RUSH:	How's it feel to be an ol' dirty banana peel with all the insides scooped out?
VIC:	Feels O.K. Care to play another game?
RUSH:	Sure. I'll beat ya worse than ever.
VIC:	You're welcome to try. Whose deal?
RUSH:	Yours.
VIC:	Toss me over the rest of the cards.
RUSH:	What's the loser hafta be this time?
VIC:	You name it.
RUSH:	How about: a bashed-in cook-stove some ol' tramp threw out in the alley?
VIC:	Excellent.
RUSH:	Hey, I'll tell ya; let's let the winner be somethin' too.
VIC:	All right.
RUSH:	What can he be?
VIC:	A dead horse that's been mean to his grand'ma an' . . . ?
RUSH:	Naw, the winner's got to be somethin' good.
VIC:	Apple pie?
RUSH:	How about fire-chief of the world with his pockets full of diamonds?

VIC: Just right. Ready for your tickets?

RUSH: Yeah.

VIC: Here they come.

RUSH: (*Chuckles*) That's pretty darn good.

VIC: What is?

RUSH: When we get through with this game, one of us'll be a bashed-in cook-stove some ol' tramp threw out in the alley, an' the other'll be fire-chief of the world with his pockets fulla diamonds.

VIC: Uh-huh.

RUSH: If you win an' get to be fire-chief of the world with your pockets fulla diamonds, you'll still be an' ol' dirty banana peel with all your insides scooped out.

VIC: I'll be quite a sight.

RUSH: An' if you lose, you'll be . . .

VIC: C'mon: your first play.

RUSH: A couple guys can have a lotta fun playin' rummy when they make up stuff to . . .

SADE: (*Entering*) Vic.

VIC: Uh-huh.

SADE: I just this minute had another set-to with Mr. Powers.

VIC: Fight?

SADE: We didn't fight, but we had a few little words. He was very snippy to me. Very snippy.

VIC: (*Mildly*) Doggone him.

SADE: Ya know what I've decided to do?

VIC: No. (*To Rush*) Hey, ya want that jack or don't ya?

RUSH: I want it but I . . .

SADE: (*Who Is Somewhat Exercised*) Be quiet a minute, son. Vic, I'm gonna tell Mr. Powers I hafta have my shed.

VIC: Make him take his bicycle out, ya mean?

SADE: Wouldn't you? When a person rents out their shed for a man to keep his bicycle in, they expect common courtesy.

VIC: What's Brother Powers been doin'?

SADE: Well, I was out on the porch just now an' . . . stop playin' cards while I tell you this.

VIC: O.K.

SADE: . . . an' he come ridin' his bicycle across the back yard big as you please. I've told him about that, ya know. Told him three or four times. Just day before yesterday he did it an' I said, "Mr. Powers, I'd prefer that you drive your bicycle up the alley instead of across the lawn."

VIC: Yeah. (*To Rush*) Hey, Stevenson, quit lookin' underneath to see what's been discarded. The rules of the game . . .

SADE: Vic, listen to me.

VIC: I'm listenin'.

SADE: An' just now it was the same thing over again. I was standin' on the porch an' here he come along on his bicycle . . . ridin' right by Mis' Fisher's fence without an "Aya," "yes," or "no."

VIC: Um.

SADE: I walked out there.

VIC: Um.

SADE: Walked right out to the shed. Mr. Powers was puttin' the lock on his bicycle. When he saw me he said, "Oh, good afternoon, Mis' Gook." I said, "Mr. Powers, I've asked you several times not to drive your bicycle across my yard." He looked at me funny an' said, "It's winter time. Don't see how I can be hurtin' any grass." "Nothing was mentioned about grass, Mr. Powers," I said. "But the ground is soft an' your bicycle wheels make deep ruts. Just step outside an' see for yourself." But he didn't move. Just stood there an' looked at me impudent for a minute. Then he said, "I guess I won't bother. I got an idea what ruts look like." Just as snippy.

VIC: He's a fiend, that guy.

SADE: Wouldn't you ask him to give up the shed?

VIC: You made the deal, Sade. He's your tenant. Do as you think best.

SADE: No reason in the world why a person should hafta

	put up with a thing like that, is there?
VIC:	None that I can see.
SADE:	Another thing he does is sit in there evenings.
VIC:	He sits in the shed evenings?
SADE:	Yes—to smoke his pipe. Mis' Harris don't allow her roomers to smoke pipes in the house, so Mr. Powers does his smokin' in the shed.
VIC:	What a heck of a place to spend your evenings.
SADE:	That's dangerous, his doin' that. Might start a fire.
VIC:	Yeah.
SADE:	Anyway I rented him that shed to keep is bicycle in—not to live in.
VIC:	The right's all on your side, Sade.
SADE:	You'd throw him out then?
VIC:	Don't know but what I would.
SADE:	(*Going*) Think I'll call him up this very evening. When a person rents out their property, they don't hafta stand for . . . (*Fades*)
VIC:	(*To Rush*) Did ya decide to keep that jack?
RUSH:	Yeah.
VIC:	All right, discard somethin' else.
RUSH:	I'll discard the deuce of spades.

VIC: Looks like Mr. Powers' bicycle's gonna lose its home.

RUSH: Yeah.

VIC: Seems a shame in a way there should be all this trouble an' heartbreak but Mr. Powers brought it on himself.

RUSH: Uh-huh—Mom won't let anybody get smart with her.

VIC: This little drama goes to show that life is made up of tears an' . . .

SADE: (*Returning*) Vic.

VIC: Yeah?

SADE: Another thing about Mr. Powers, he's way behind in his rent.

VIC: Is he?

SADE: Moved his bicycle in the shed the first of August, paid me for one month, an' never come across with one red cent since.

VIC: As I remember it, the rental on our shed is very low too.

SADE: Fifteen cents is all.

VIC: Fifteen cents a month?

SADE: Yeah.

VIC: (*Laughs*)

SADE: What's the matter?

VIC: That is low rent.

SADE: 'Course it is. It's about right, though. A person can rent a garage for their auto for three dollars a month. Fifteen cents for a bicycle in a shed makes it just about fair.

VIC: (*Chuckles*) Uh-huh. An' Mr. Powers has only paid you for one month?

SADE: Just one little fifteen cents. Paid him up through August. He owes for all of September, all of October, an' half of November. How much does that make?

VIC: Makes . . . a . . . thirty-seven an' a half cents.

SADE: Call it thirty-seven.

VIC: O.K.

SADE: He's thirty-seven cents behind in his rent, he drives his bicycle over my yard, he's snippy with me, an' he uses the shed to sit in evenings. Don't you think I'm justified in throwin' him out?

VIC: (*Judiciously*) Yes, I believe I do.

SADE: I'll call him up right after supper. What'd I better say: "Mr. Powers, I must ask you for the wood-shed"?

VIC: Uh-huh.

SADE: Or shall I say, 'Mr. Powers, under the circumstances, I must ask you for the wood-shed.'?

VIC:	Either one sounds O.K.
SADE:	Ya don't s'pose he'll get mad an' fly into a tantrum?
VIC:	Naw. Guys get thrown outa places every day in the week. Anyway he richly deserves harsh treatment.
SADE:	I don't care if he does get mad. I'll say, "Mr. Powers, you haven't been at all satisfactory in my shed. You've driven your bicycle across my yard after I asked you not to, an' you haven't talked to me the way I'm used to being talked to."
VIC:	Yeah.
SADE:	When had I better tell him to vacate . . . first of December?
VIC:	Be a good time.
SADE:	See this is the sixteenth of November. Can't hardly make him get out in the middle of the month.
VIC:	No.
SADE:	First of December'll give him two weeks to remove his bicycle.
RUSH:	(*Laughs*)
SADE:	(*Sharply*) What's the matter with you?
RUSH:	Sounded kinda funny what you said. It don't take a guy two weeks to move a little bicycle out of . . .
SADE:	That'll be enough, son. I'll tell him that then, huh, Vic? I'll say, "Mr. Powers, I must ask you for the wood-shed on the first of December."

VIC: Yeah.

SADE: (*Her Soft Heart Asserting Itself*) You . . . you don't think I'm doing wrong, do you?

VIC: Not at all.

SADE: Well, I don't like to have trouble with people.

VIC: You're doin' exactly the right thing.

SADE: (*Going*) I'll call him after a while then. A person can't let themselves be run over by other people when . . . (*Fades*)

VIC: (*To Rush*) Whose move?

RUSH: Yours.

VIC: I'll snag onto this Queen.

RUSH: Remember what the loser an' winners' gonna be?

VIC: To be absolutely certain I oughta have my memory refreshed.

RUSH: Loser's gonna be a bashed-in cook-stove some ol' tramp threw out in the alley. Winner's gonna be fire-chief of the world with his pockets full of diamonds.

VIC: To be sure.

RUSH: Wonder where Mr. Powers is gonna keep his bicycle now.

VIC: Let's not think about the sad aspects of this tragic business, Pete. Mr. Powers is a wicked man who . . .

SADE: (*Returning*) Vic, would you say anything about the thirty-seven cents?

VIC: Huh?

SADE: When I call up Mr. Powers had I better mention the back rent?

VIC: He owes it to ya.

SADE: Yes, but I hate to . . . I don't wanta be too hard on him all at a clatter.

VIC: I'd dun him for it.

SADE: Would, huh?

VIC: Sure I would.

SADE: Well, maybe I could . . . kinda give him a discount. Maybe only ask thirty-five cents. Or twenty-five.

VIC: Whatever you think best.

SADE: Vic, another thing I thought of was Mr. Powers was in jail one time.

VIC: Yeah?

SADE: He got in a fight an' smashed a fella in the nose, an' the fella had him put behind bars.

VIC: When was all that?

SADE: Oh, a long time ago. But it does make kind of a bad reputation.

VIC: Uh-huh.

SADE: (*Building Up A Case Against Mr. Powers*) Person oughta be good an' careful who they have around their property, don'tcha think?

VIC: Darn right. No use rentin' out your wood-shed to a jail-bird.

SADE: You . . . you really think I oughta throw him out, huh?

VIC: Sure.

SADE: After all it's not like throwin' him out on the street personally. Just his bicycle.

VIC: That's right.

SADE: Well, I . . . I think I'll call him up right now. Get it over with.

VIC: Go ahead.

SADE: Gracious, but I hate unpleasant things like this.

VIC: A human being's got to take the bitter with the sweet.

SADE: (*Off A Little*) I'll say, "Mr. Powers, I must ask you for the wood-shed on December first," huh?

VIC: Yeah.

SADE: (*To Phone*) 2379-J, please. Yes. (*To Vic*) Hope this don't spoil his evening or anything.

VIC: You're too soft-hearted, kiddo. (*Chuckles*) Heck, I been kicked outa . . .

SADE: (*To Phone*) Hello, Mis' Harris? This is Mis' Gook. Yes. Say, is Mr. Powers there? Well, may I speak to him, please? Thank you. (*To Vic*) She's gonna call him.

VIC: He little knows the fate that awaits him.

SADE: Poor fella.

VIC: Why poor fella?

SADE: Mr. Powers is really not a bad man. Just one of those harum-scarum sorta . . . (*To Phone*) Hello, Mr. Powers? This is Mis' Gook, Mr. Powers. Yes. Say, Mr. Powers, I'm . . . I'm very sorry, but I'm afraid I'll hafta ask you to give up the bicycle . . . I mean the wood-shed on December . . . What? Talk louder? (*Louder*) I say I'm very sorry but I'm afraid I'll hafta ask you to . . . What? Well, I don't see why you can't hear me. I'm talking loud. I say, Mr. Powers, I'd like to have my wood-shed on December first. Yes. Well . . . because . . . of . . . of circumstances. Yes. I don't think you've acted just the way . . . what? (*To The Others*) Know what he's doin'?

VIC & RUSH: What?

SADE: Pretending to cry.

VIC & RUSH: Cry?

SADE: Just boo-hooin' away. (*To Phone*) There's no call for any foolishness like that, Mr. Powers. If you feel that . . . What? What'll become of your poor little bicycle now? I'm serious about this. I'd appreciate it very much if you'd vacate the first of . . . What? You will? Thank you very much, Mr. Powers. I'm sorry things didn't turn out . . . What? All right then. All right then, Mr. Powers. Good-by.

(*Hangs Up*)

Vic: Did he say he'd get out?

Sade: Yes.

Vic: Did he sound very sad?

Sade: No. Such a smart-aleck he is. Said he'd get out December first like I asked, but he'd rather not talk about it any more now. His heart was too full.

Rush: Shucks.

Sade: You really think I done the right thing, Vic?

Vic: Sure.

Sade: It oughta be easy for him to find another place for his bicycle.

Vic: Of course.

Sade: (*Going*) Well, I'm glad it's over. I can't abide trouble an' hard feelings with people. I like to have everything smooth an' . . . (*Fade*)

Vic: (*To Rush*) Whose play?

Rush: Yours.

VIC: I'll take this King of hearts. An' with this King of hearts I expect to . . . Whatcha laughin' at?

RUSH: What you laughin' at?

VIC: Oh, this an' that.

RUSH: I'm laughin' at this an' that too.

VIC: Well, let's not hold up the game. I've played. It's your turn. Shoot.

END OF SCRIPT

ANNOUNCER: Vic, Sade, and young Rush invite you to tune in for them every time they're on the air. They'd like to think of you as regular members of their family circle.

February 11, 1958

Dear Bill:

I telephoned both Bernardine and Peggy about your mother. I think you would have been touched by the anecdotes they told me—all warm unplanned tributes to a valiant, aggressive, intensely family-minded woman who had won their affection and respect. Mary Fran had some fancy things to say too. She may write and tell them to you her own self.

Bernardine listened to me read your entire letter when I gave her the blast on the tubes and I could sense that she was affronted and sickened by your gross sex talk with its revolting allusions to oriental customs dealing with devices to make a man scream while coming. Take a little tip, Bill: leave smut out of your letters. I myself have made it a rule never to soil my correspondence with anything questionable, vulgar, or tasteless. I feel strongly on the subject and have always had the feeling that a man who would descend to loose undisciplined language is no better than sock of shit.

VIC AND SADE   (*Crisco*)

GRANDPA SNYDER'S MEDICINE   DECEMBER 11, 1934   TUESDAY

ANNOUNCER: OPENING AND COMMERCIAL CREDITS

INTRODUCTION: It is late afternoon as our scene opens now, and here in the kitchen we find Rush all by himself. The young man is bending over the table, upon the top of which is arrayed an impressive assortment of bottles, boxes, and dishes. We can't imagine what on earth the boy is up to, but . . . Wait a second, here's a newcomer just entering the back door. It's Vic. And he says to his son . . .

VIC: Hi.

RUSH: H'lo, Gov.

VIC: Whatcha gonna do—start a drug store?

RUSH: No. I got a job.

VIC: Job?

RUSH: Gonna spend this evening over at Gran'pa Snyder's house givin' him his medicine.

VIC: Does all that junk comprise his medicine?

RUSH: Lot of it, ain't there? Well, he's a pretty old geezer. Needs a lotta stuff.

VIC: How come ya got his medicine here at home?

RUSH: I'm studyin' up on the different doses. Got his chart, see? The way I got the job, Gran'pa Snyder's two daughters are going to an entertainment at the

	High School tonight. They hired me to come over from six-thirty till ten an' take care of Gran'pa. Pretty good job too. I'm gonna get fifty cents.
VIC:	What's in this box?
RUSH:	Pills, I expect. What's it say on the lid?
VIC:	(*Reads*) 'Yamilton's Drug Department. H-97-Z-124.'
RUSH:	I'll look it up on the chart. H-97-Z-124?
VIC:	Yeah.
RUSH:	(*Reads*) Give Gran'pa two of these with a glass of water twenty minutes after eating and at half hour intervals after that.
VIC:	Hmm. What's this?
RUSH:	I dunno. It's just called "blue stuff" on the chart. (*Reads*) Give Gran'pa level teaspoonful of blue stuff every two hours beginning at six-thirty.
VIC:	I s'pose the villainous lookin' brew in this bottle is referred to as yella stuff.
RUSH:	Uh-huh. (**Consults Chart**) Give Gran'pa tablespoonful of yella stuff at twenty-five minutes to nine.
VIC:	Looks to me like there's enough junk here to doctor up an army.
RUSH:	Plenty of it all right. Well, you take an old guy like that, they hafta have . . .
VIC:	What's this thing?

RUSH: It's just kind of a flat dish.

VIC: Gran'pa Snyder gonna swallow it with a glass of water at midnight?

RUSH: (*Laughs*) Naw. See this box?

VIC: Yeah.

RUSH: It's got powder in it. I put the powder in a pan with water. Then I heat the water. Then I pour the water in that flat dish an' Gran'pa inhales the fumes.

VIC: Gran'pa must put in some lively evenings.

RUSH: (*Laughs*) Yeah. I wouldn't wanta hafta take such a bunch of medicine. Maybe when I get old though I'll . . .

VIC: What's this black stuff?

RUSH: I dunno. (*Consults Chart*) Give Gran'pa one pinch of black stuff twelve minutes after he eats his egg.

VIC: What time does he eat his egg?

RUSH: Ah . . . (*Reads*) Give Gran'pa one raw egg at nine-fifteen.

VIC: What if he don't feel like an egg?

RUSH: I thought of that myself. If he turned down the doggone egg it'd throw the whole works off. Some other things I gotta find out about too. Look here for instance: "Give Gran'pa pink stuff at hour-and-a-half intervals beginning at six-fifty-three." This here is the pink stuff, ya see?

Vic:	Uh-huh.
Rush:	Well—an' hour an' a half from six-fifty-three would be an hour plus six-fifty-three or seven-fifty-three plus a half hour makin' it eight-twenty-three. That's the first interval. O.K. Eight-twenty-three plus an' hour an' a half would be an hour plus eight-twenty-three or nine-twenty-three plus a half hour makin' it . . .
Vic:	Holy smoke.
Rush:	See how mixed up it is?
Vic:	You better take an adding machine along. An' a private secretary.
Rush:	An' another thing. I hafta give Gran'pa his X-26-Y-14 pills at eight-twenty-four. That'd only give me a minute gangway between the pink stuff an' the . . .
Vic:	I think you better resign from that job.
Rush:	Oh, no. I can use that fifty cents. Anyway, pretty soon I'll call up one of the Snyder girls an' get everything straight in my mind.
Vic:	Here's a bottle that says, "take two or three pills every three or four hours."
Rush:	Yeah. What's a guy gonna do about that?
Vic:	Why dontcha mix all this stuff up in a jug, an' give it to Gran'pa in one big snort?
Rush:	He'd prob'ly explode. (*They Laugh*) No, I think I'll make out a list of questions an' then call the Snyder residence on the phone. Ask one of the girls . . .

VIC: I believe your mother is coming up the back steps.

At this point Sade enters with a lot of packages. She's been Christmas shopping and she wants to show Vic all her purchases. She opens the packages and chatters about who they're for and why she bought them while Rush continues to puzzle over his problem.

❖ ❖ ❖ ❖

RUSH: Gov, I'm gonna run into plenty of trouble at eight-forty-six tonight.

VIC: How so?

RUSH: Well, three different medicines conflict at eight-forty-six. Unless I have a stop-watch, I'll probably . . .

❖ ❖ ❖ ❖

RUSH: Know what I'm gonna hafta do, Gov?

VIC: What?

RUSH: Make out kind of a time-table like they have on the railroad. If I don't I'll have Gran'pa Snyder's stomach so upside-down he won't know . . .

SADE: (*Giggles*) Vic, look . . .

VIC: Don't recognize it.

SADE: (*Giggles Wickedly*) I don't s'pose I should do this, but Bess'll never know the difference.

VIC: What is it?

SADE: It's perfume. Sample.

VIC:	Sample of perfume?
SADE:	Yes. I had the girl take off the label that said sample. See Bess is crazy about perfume but she'd rather jump over the moon than buy any . . . Thinks it's so extravagant. Thought I'd tuck it in with her main present.
VIC:	Uh-huh.
SADE:	Think that's a terrible thing to do—give somebody a sample of something for Christmas?
VIC:	It's O.K. I guess. Well, believe I'll go in the other room an' . . .
SADE:	No, stay an' see the rest of my presents. Rush, you lookin' too?
RUSH:	I'm busy studyin' this medicine chart. Gov, I found some more tough goin'. Remember that egg I'm s'posed to give Gran'pa at nine-fifteen?
VIC:	Yeah.
RUSH:	It sure gums up the works. He's got a shot of black stuff comin' at the same time, an' also two pills to be given with a glass of water.
VIC:	Make him an egg-nogg. Blindfold him an' . . .
SADE:	This is for Herman Grably, Vic.
VIC:	Handkerchief?
SADE:	Yes, an' a ten-center at that. Well, he can't expect much. The way he acted at the picnic.

VIC: Why send him anything?

SADE: Oh, you just can't up an' leave people out altogether. Herman'll get his little handkerchief an' . . . Got this for Mis' Brighton.

VIC: Fish dish?

SADE: Nut meat boat.

VIC: Huh?

SADE: Nut meat boat. You put your nut meats in it. Latest thing in the city. I really wouldn't hafta give to Mis' Brighton, but after all she's the head of the Thimble an' . . . Oh, say, wanta show ya somethin' else cute.

RUSH: Gov, if ya say pills are to be taken twenty minutes after supper, do ya meant twenty minutes after you finished supper or twenty minutes after ya started supper?

VIC: Finished supper, I should imagine. If ya took 'em twenty mintues from the time you started supper, an' your supper lasted thirty minutes, you'd be takin' pills along with your pun'kin pie an' . . .

SADE: (*Giggles*) Here, Vic.

VIC: What's that?

SADE: Little bottles of candy drops for the twins. Ain't they sweet?

VIC: Yeah.

SADE: I'm really givin' 'em gloves, but they wouldn't think it was Christmas unless they get some little

Vic:	knick-knack. So I'll stick these little bottles up inside the gloves. Catch on?
	Uh-huh.
Rush:	If Gran'pa should hafta leave the room for more than five minutes at a crack, It'd throw my whole schedule clear outa . . .
Sade:	Little dollar shaving outfit for Fred.
Vic:	Um.
Sade:	Cheap cigars for Gran'pa. (*To Defend Their Cheapness*) He only breaks 'em up an' smokes 'em in his pipe, ya know.
Vic:	Uh-huh.
Rush:	Gov, if ya add one hour an' thirty-three minutes to two hours an' eleven minutes, an' it's five-twelve o'clock an' eighteen seconds when ya . . .
Sade:	Vic.
Vic:	Yeah.
Sade:	Here's a little bottle of hand-cream I had 'em make up special. Same kind Ruthie uses. I thought I'd get myself a real fancy flask in the jewelry department an' . . . Whatcha doin', son?
Rush:	Puttin' all this medicine back in the basket. I'm going over to Snyder's an' ask a thousand questions about . . .
Sade:	Don't put my perfume sample in your basket.

RUSH: What perfume sample?

SADE: This. Give it here.

RUSH: That's Gran'pa Snyder's blue stuff, Mom.

SADE: It is not. It's . . .

RUSH: This must be your perfume sample.

SADE: No that's my hand cream.

RUSH: We're both wrong, Mom. That's Gran'pa's yella stuff.

SADE: I just this minute laid it on the table. Didn't I, Vic?

VIC: Couldn't prove it by me. I got nothing to do with . . .

RUSH: Here's your hand cream.

SADE: Is it?

RUSH: Unless . . . unless it's Gran'pa Snyder's yella stuff.

SADE: Well, if this don't beat the Dutch.

RUSH: Wasn't my fault, Mom. We both had out stuff here on the table an' . . .

SADE: Think I'm gonna give Bess medicine to use for hand cream?

RUSH: I certainly don't wanta give Gran'pa Snyder hand cream for medicine.

SADE: Ya got the twins' little bottles of candy drops in your basket too.

RUSH:	Naw—those are Gran'pa Snyder's pills.
SADE:	What are these then?
RUSH:	I . . . I don't know.
SADE:	Is this my perfume?
RUSH:	Yeah. Unless it's Gran'pa Snyder's blue stuff.
SADE:	Vic.
VIC:	What?
SADE:	What shall we do?

END OF SCRIPT

ANNOUNCER: Yes, Vic—what shall we do? (*Pause*)

COMMERCIALS AND CLOSING

CALVIN COOLIDGE:	Why is it that nature has fixed it so the human turd is tapered?
JOHNNY COONS:	I give up.
CALVIN COOLIDGE:	It keeps your ass-hole from clanging shut.

On December 17th, as Christmas drew near, Paul wrote one of those typical Rhymer scripts that demonstrated his ingenious plot mind and also his philosophical and psychological insight.

Rush comes home wearing Rooster Davis' pants, which are ripped badly in the seat. Rooster is waiting out in the woodshed, wearing Rush's pants, while Rush has Sade repair his own. See, Rooster would have been too embarrassed to come into the house himself wearing the ripped pants, so Rush gallantly traded pants with Rooster until Rooster's are fixed. Anyway, while the repairs are going on, Rush discovers some disturbing items in Rooster's pants pockets:

❖ ❖ ❖ ❖

SADE: Rush, give me those pants.

RUSH: Here. Gov, wouldn't you jump down that guy's throat?

VIC: Don't know but what I would.

RUSH: Here I was doin' him a favor: lettin' him sit in my own woodshed while my own Mother sewed up his darn ol' pants. An' all the time he had this evidence in his pockets: piece of green chalk he wrote on my back with an' said he didn't: eleven cents in cash when he's owed me three cents for six weeks: ink-eraser he copped offa me; an' a note to Mildred Tisdel when he knows I'm the guy she walks home with when she don't walk home with the girls.

VIC: A black unbelievable story.

RUSH: Just wait'll I get him.

VIC: Did you find anything incriminating in those other articles there?

RUSH: No.

VIC: What are those other articles?

RUSH: Just junk Rooster carries in his pocket: little book about how to fix your cook-stove: comb with all the teeth out; busted fountain pen; hinge off a screen door; heel-plate; lady's shoe button; huntin'

	license good in Ohio in 1914; horse-shoe nail . . . just different stuff.
SADE:	Here's the pants, son—all fixed.
RUSH:	Thank you very much, Mom.
SADE:	Tell Rooster to look out for nails in telephone poles after this.
RUSH:	Yeah. Say, guess I'll put these pants on. Trade with Rooster out in the shed.

❖ ❖ ❖ ❖

VIC:	(*Chuckles*) He'll prob'ly get warmed up when Rush takes that poke at him.
SADE:	I don't think he'll take any poke at Rooster. Tried it twice before an' come out the dirty end of the stick. (*Giggles*) Was kinda funny them things in the pants pocket.
VIC:	Uh-huh. Wonder what I'd find if I went through my best friend's clothes.
SADE:	It's kinda like that business about eavesdroppers seldom hear good of themselves.
VIC:	Uh-huh. After all the contents of a man's pants pocket are . . . (*Door Opens*)
RUSH:	(*Entering*) I forgot my overcoat.
SADE:	Yes. There on the chair.
VIC:	Changed pants yet?

RUSH: No. We decided to wear each other's pants the rest of the morning. Awful cold out in that shed. Rooster says thanks, Mom.

SADE: Tell him glad to help.

RUSH: (*Moving Off*) Well—see ya at dinner time.

VIC: Oh, son, did you take that poke at Rooster?

RUSH: No, I didn't. We . . . we kinda fixed things up.

VIC: How so?

RUSH: Well . . . a . . . ya see, he had my pants on just now?

VIC: Uh-huh.

RUSH: An' he got to monkeyin' around an' found some stuff in my pockets.

VIC: What'd he find?

RUSH: Oh—just a few different articles.

VIC: What were they?

RUSH: A buffalo nickel with a hole in it I swiped off him, an' a little tube of mucilage that gave it away I was the guy that stuck his arithmetic book to his geography book, an' a piece of wire just like the piece of wire somebody tied his overshoes together with, an' a bottle of red sand like the red sand he found in his hat at school the other day.

VIC: Oh.

Rush:	So we . . . we kinda fixed it up.
Vic:	Uh-huh.
Rush:	I agreed to overlook what I found in his pockets, an' he agreed to overlook what he found in my pockets.
Vic:	I see.
Rush:	Well, I'll get on to school now. (*Moves Off*) So long, Gov.
Vic:	So long.
Rush:	So long, Mom.
Sade:	So long.
Rush:	(*Opens Door*) See ya at dinner time.
Sade:	Uh-huh.
Rush:	Good-by. (*Closes Door*)

End of Script

Announcer:	Which concludes a tale of torn pants, revealing pockets, storm, threats, heart-break, and the final reconciliation of two friends. (*Pause*)

Commercials and Closing

Peggy asked me over recently to go through a bureau drawer of Art's containing material having to do with the program. She also offered me Art's gold watch as a keepsake. I accepted it gratefully.

Chapter Eight — 1935

The nineteenth floor of the Merchandise Mart (NBC) was a very busy place. So, also, were the studios in the Wrigley Building (CBS) and across the street in the Tribune Tower (WGN), which became part of the Mutual Network. For Chicago was the center of the radio business. Some of the big nighttime shows which featured stars of the movies and the stage were done in New York and Los Angeles, but the bulk of radio, nighttime as well as daytime, came from Chicago.

It was a good racket for the performers. Almost everyone who was any good at all could make a living, and a lot of people got rich. You'd see actors in the lobby of NBC rushing by with scripts stuck in every pocket, going from one show to another. Van, Bern and I all worked other shows; at one time I had parts in six regular radio series!

But Chicago radio people had a very special attitude. They were in show business and yet somehow not of it. They actually sneered at the actors and actresses that worked in Hollywood and on Broadway. To the Chicago radio folk, those other actors still bore the stigma of theatrical people in olden times. They were not quite respectable.

To the Chicago radio people, the rest of show business was somehow tawdry and childish. This superior feeling was probably held by all radio people to some extent, but it was especially true of the ones from Chicago, since those in New York had some association with Broadway and the ones in California often doubled in pictures. But the Chicago people had no other such influence. Radio was king there and it was all, and the Chicago radio folks were something of a breed apart.

They felt their ability to do radio was a highly sophisticated skill. It certainly was a trick not easily done by all actors. To do everything with voice alone, to read scripts cold. And to do a performance with an hour or two preparation, while reading from a script. It took a tremendous amount of facility. Actors in Hollywood who got days to do a few line and those on Broadway who rehearsed weeks to do a play were considered a lower grade of human being. And this assessment received reinforcement if not proof when these Broadway or Hollywood creatures appeared in Chicago to do a radio show. Usually they fumbled over their lines, sounded wooden and amateurish, and were often immobilized with fright. The Chicago radio actors would smile behind their backs and exchange knowing looks. We were the cream of show business, we felt. Anyone could do pictures and theatre; it took a special sort of person to do radio. And we were right, in a way, I guess. Unfortunately, when radio folded we found our special skills didn't count for much, and the actors we'd previously held in contempt were the ones who worked.

Vic and Sade's marriage portrait.

But while it lasted the radio people lived good lives. An established radio actor in Chicago had a nice house in one of the suburbs, a nice car, a family. He was like a businessman. He went down to work in the morning and came home to a life full of leisure hours (no studying of lines). He did quite a bit of drinking, usually, although fairly well-controlled. He had a regular set of friends. He lived regular hours, had a work shop in his garage and snickered at the stories of life in Hollywood. Perhaps secretly he might like a little of that wild life himself, but openly he was above it. For ten or twelve years this group of radio people lived this stable, pleasant, utterly respectable, business-like existence.

So it was somehow right and proper that Vic and Sade, which epitomized niceness and respectability, was done in Chicago; perhaps it was the only place it could have been done well, because it was so much a part of the middle-west: middle-west show business as well as middle-west life. It all went together.

In 1935 Rush was in the eighth grade at Edwards school—the graduating class. In the fall he would be going to high school. He was making the transition from childhood to adolescence and this furnished Paul with one of his major themes for this year. He turned his attention from Vic to Rush and explored the boy at this complex time of his life. Again, one can only marvel at the tremendous awareness and retention of the feelings and happenings of the extravagant phase of our lives, and the way Paul handled them for artistic effect.

The kids are supposed to come up with a class motto—a last word to be left behind from the graduating class of '35. Rush comes home with the problem and tries to get Vic to help:

❖ ❖ ❖ ❖

VIC: How about this: "Edwards School, dear alma mater, never shall I forget thy teaching."

RUSH: No soap.

VIC: Why not?

RUSH: The graduating class of nineteen-thirty had one just like it.

VIC: No foolin'?

RUSH: Almost like it. They had, "Edwards School, blessed alma mater, they teachings sleep within my brain."

VIC: Sleep within my brain?

RUSH: Yeah. Hot stuff, huh?

VIC: That "sleep" in there sounds like the guy forgot everything he learned at Edwards School.

RUSH: Yeah, but that don't cut no ice. Just so the motto sounds good is all that makes any difference.

VIC: I see. Well, whatcha think of this: "Non disputandum esse nihil omnibus ho."

RUSH: What's that mean?

VIC: "Let us pluck the raspberries from the top of the tree."

RUSH: Don't sound like much of a motto.

VIC: It's a good motto. Got an allergorical significance. It advises a man not to lazily pluck the raspberries that lay upon the ground, but to gird his loins an' climb higher and higher.

❖ ❖ ❖ ❖

JOKE

RAYMOND: What were you doing in that sidewalk café last night?

HAROLD: That wasn't any sidewalk café, that was my furniture.

A few days later Rush and Rooster start out to go downtown and watch a guy eat raw fish in the window of the Greek's (advertising stunt) but stop at Mildred's and she sells them on an idea. He comes home wanting to go upstairs into the attic and get some of his old toys from the green trunk that's up there:

MILDRED TISDEL'S IDEA   January 7, 1935

SADE: You want to play with those little baby toys?

RUSH: Not exactly play with 'em.

SADE: What do you want with 'em?

RUSH: I want 'em to . . . O.K., I'll tell you Mildred Tisdel's idea.

SADE: All right.

RUSH: Don't laugh, Gov.

VIC: All right.

RUSH: Mildred's idea sounds kinda crazy, but she sold me an' Rooster on it an' we decided it was worth tryin'.

VIC: Whip out the details.

RUSH: Well, it's . . . a . . . kinda of a game ya play with yourself.

VIC: I see.

RUSH: A game to make yourself sad.

SADE: Oh, my, my, my.

RUSH: Don't get disgusted till I make it clear to ya, Mom. Here's the angle: I want them toys that's in the attic to look at—an' feel melancholy about my happy childhood that I'll never see again.

SADE: Heavens alive!

RUSH: According to Mildred a person can get a dandy sad feelin' doin' that. You know the kind of a sad feelin' I mean. The kind ya get in movie shows where somebody dies, ya know.

SADE: Um.

RUSH: You catch on to what I'm trying to get across, don't you, Gov?

VIC: Just barely.

RUSH: You've felt sorry for yourself, haven't ya, an' got a thrill out of it?

VIC: Sure.

RUSH: Well, that's Mildred's idea in a nut-shell. I know it sounds dumb, but ya oughta see her go to town on it. Why, right in the personal presence of Rooster Davis an' me she whipped out great big tears.

VIC: Thinkin' about her happy childhood she'll never see again?

RUSH: Sure. She had one of her baby shoes in her hand, see, an' she was sayin', "Oh, if I could only once more grovel on the floor so sweet an' curly-headed."

SADE: Rush, I think Mildred an' Rooster an' the whole caboodle of you kids are a little ding-bats.

It is delirious news about your visiting Chicago. Mary Fran has arranged several excursions for you. She has gathered together half a dozen lads of your age and the idea is to pack sandwiches and hike to various places of interest here and there about the city. The lilacs are blooming at Brookfield Zoo. The Aquarium has much to attract the Chicago visitor and just standing on one of our busy corners and watching the traffic is a thrill. I personally have an excursion planned for just the two of us where we go to Washington Park (which opens today) and drink eleven martinis and lose four hundred dollars and ogle the girls and finally fall down.

Of course Rush's transition to puberty was not the only theme of the show at this time. As usual, the scripts ranged over the whole spectrum of small-town life as seen by Rhymer. For instance, January 22 is apparently Mr. Gumpox, the garbage man's, birthday. Sade found out today, quite by accident, from Mrs. Henderson, and hasn't had time to get a gift or anything, and, as luck would have it, this also happens to be the day Mr. Gumpox comes by . . .

MR. GUMPOX'S BIRTHDAY PRESENT   JANUARY 22, 1935

SADE: Well, let's hurry up quick an' think of something. He won't be by for another week. Rush, you got anything in mind we could give?

RUSH: No.

SADE: Well, think. Remember Mr. Gumpox's been awful good to you. Fixed your bicycle an' let you ride on his garbage wagon.

RUSH: That was no treat. I went over to see Mildred afterwards an' she said by gosh who let the skunk loose. I felt like thirty cents an' tried to let on like there'd been an explosion down at the slaughter house an' . . .

SADE: Vic, how about them socks you got?

VIC: Which ones?

SADE: The ones John an' Lucille sent. They're up in your drawer, ain't they?

VIC: Yeah, but Mr. Gumpox wouldn't wear them.

SADE: Why not?

VIC: If he's got any self-respect he wouldn't. They're those doggone white college socks with the little footballs embroidered on 'em.

SADE: I think they'd be all right. They're good heavy woolen socks. After all it's the idea of givin' a birthday present. Rush, will ya run upstairs?

RUSH: An' get them funny socks with the . . .

SADE: Yes. Hurry.

RUSH: Sometimes Mr. Gumpox don't wear socks. That day I rode with him he . . .

SADE: Go do like I say. Vic, know what might be nice?

VIC: Dinner?

SADE: We'll eat in a minute. Listen, how'd it be to lay our little present out beside the garbage bucket?

VIC:	He might not see it.
SADE:	We'll write 'Happy Birthday' on a piece of paper an' tie it to the bucket.
VIC:	He'll think we're givin' him garbage for his birthday.
SADE:	He won't think any such thing. Tell ya what: there's an empty cigar box in the pantry. I'll wrap the socks up nice in it.
VIC:	All right.
SADE:	Got a pencil an' a piece of paper?
VIC:	Got a pencil.
SADE:	Give it here.
VIC:	Why not put the present in the garbage? Then, all unknowing when he sorts out his garbage at the end of the day, his heart will be made glad to discover . . .
SADE:	You got no piece of paper, huh?
VIC:	No
SADE:	(*Calls*) Rush.
RUSH:	(*Off*) Yeah?
SADE:	Out of the library table drawer get my tablet an' a long envelope.
RUSH:	(*Off*) O.K.

SADE: Think I'll write a little note. Say somethin' like . . . a . . . in appreciation of your kindness an' . . . an' . . . What could I say?

VIC: Write a poem. Say . . . a . . . "Oh, garbage man. O, garbage man. I've put my faith in thee. Your lovely face, your dark brown eyes are sweet as sweet can be. An' when the sun begins to sink, into the golden west, my heart leaps up an' I behold . . ."

SADE: (*Somewhat Tartly*) You can sit down an' start to eat if ya want to.

VIC: An invitation I'm prompt to accept.

SADE: Person might give a person a little help.

VIC: I'll be more than glad to offer my services in the interests of . . .

RUSH: (*Returning*) Dinner ready?

SADE: You can sit down. Got the socks?

RUSH: Yeah. They're in a Christmas box though. Mr. Gumpox might think . . .

SADE: Before you sit down go in the pantry an' get that cigar box on the shelf.

RUSH: I planned to make somethin' outa that cigar box. I . . .

SADE: Do like I say. Where's the things from the library table?

RUSH: Here.

SADE: All right. Go get the cigar box.

RUSH: I been savin' that cigar box. I . . . (*Moving Off*)

SADE: Look out an' see if the garbage buckets are still there.

RUSH: (*Off A Little*) They're there.

SADE: (*To Vic*) What shall I write on the envelope? Happy birthday Mr. Gumpox?

VIC: Yeah. Or better still:—"Bright star, would I were steadfast as thou art. Hung aloft the dark canopy of night like . . ."

SADE: (*With Some Acid*) I'll fix it. Person could break their back doin' favors for a person an' a person'd never give a care.

VIC: You misunderstand, Mrs. Craig. The relations between Mr. Gumpox an' myself . . .

RUSH: (*Back Again*) Maybe I could get this cigar box back again, Mom. After Mr. Gumpox gets his socks, he won't have any use for . . .

SADE: Lay it down.

RUSH: Watcha writin'?

SADE: (*Briefly*) Note.

RUSH: Gonna put the present in the garbage?

SADE: Sit down an' eat your dinner.

RUSH: (*Laughs*) Gov, is Mom gonna put the present in the garbage?

VIC:	I couldn't say.
RUSH:	Know what'd be funny?
VIC:	What?
RUSH:	Give Mr. Gumpox a piece of pie for his birthday an' put it in the garbage. He wouldn't know which was his present an' which was . . . (*Himself And His Villainous Father Hugely Enjoy This Notion*)
SADE:	Some people can be just awful silly over nothin'.
VIC:	Ya hear that last crack by the doctor here?
SADE:	Yes, I did. Ridiculous nonsense for a great big boy in the eighth grade.
VIC:	Sure is. I got an idea, Polo.
RUSH:	What?
VIC:	Say Mr. Gumpox is fifty years old.
RUSH:	(*Prepared To Laugh*) Yeah.
VIC:	How about stickin' fifty candles around in the garbage bucket?
RUSH:	Make it look like a cake, huh? (*They Laugh At This*)
SADE:	Oh, stop that foolishness for goodness sake. Vic, how's this? (*Reads*) Dear Mr. Gumpox. Just a little remembrance on your birthday. Good luck an' many more of 'em. The Gook Family. All right?
VIC:	Fine.

SADE: I'll get some nice white paper an' . . . LISTEN

VIC: What?

SADE: Heard wagon wheels. Rush, look quick an' see if . . .

RUSH: He's at Harris' house.

SADE: Oh, my. Well, look, run out with these. We won't bother with the cigar box. Hurry now.

RUSH: (*Getting Up*) Shall I put the present in the garbage?

SADE: Put it beside the garbage. Put the envelope with the note on top of the garbage. Scoot.

RUSH: (*Opens Door*) O.K.

SADE: (*After Him*) Try not to let him see you.

RUSH: O.K. (*Closes Door*)

SADE: Let's go to the window.

VIC: I'm busy with cabbage.

SADE: C'mon—see what he does.

VIC: (*Getting Up*) Maybe he'll swoon. Maybe he'll try on his socks an' . . .

SADE: (*Off A Little*) Rush is certainly a good fast runner. Out there already.

VIC: Well, heaven lends wings to the feet of those who run on blessed missions. "Beautiful feet are those that go. On kindly errands to and fro."

SADE: Mr. Gumpox is headin' for our buckets again.

VIC: Did he see Rush?

SADE: Rush is almost up on the porch again.

VIC: Make it snappy, Gumpox.

SADE: There—he sees the envelope.

VIC: Uh-huh. Be unfortunate if he couldn't read. Mr. Gumpox, though a man of sterling character . . . (*Door Opens*)

RUSH: (*Off*) He's readin' the note, Mom.

SADE: Yeah—we're watchin' him.

RUSH: Don't think he even saw me.

VIC: You're no breathless vision even if he did . . .

RUSH: (*Up*) Move over, Gov.

SADE: He's opening his present. Vic, he's opening his present.

VIC: Uh-huh.

RUSH: I can't see nothin'. Shove over, Gov.

SADE: He's got it open. There's the socks.

VIC: (*Chuckles*) Little footballs embroidered on . . .

RUSH: C'mon, Gov, give a guy room.

SADE: Vic, he's lookin' up here an' smilin'. Open the window.

VIC:	Aw, shucks, there's no necessity for . . .
SADE:	He sees us. Open the window.
VIC:	(*Opening It*) Give me gang-way then. (*Grunts*)
SADE:	All right. Get outa the way, son. (*Calls*) Happy Birthday, Mr. Gumpox. Happy Birthday.

END OF SCRIPT

ANNOUNCER:	Yes, Mr. Gumpox, happy birthday.

COMMERCIALS AND CLOSING

JOKE:	A druggist got off to a bad day. He stumbled over his alarm clock getting out of bed and hurt his toe something fierce. He cut himself shaving and had a painful and unsatisfactory bowel movement. His wife was evil-tempered at breakfast and his eggs were underdone and slightly stale. Leaving the house he tripped over his kid's roller skate and almost broke his back. Arriving at his drug store he saw that hoodlums had thrown a brick through his plate glass window. The phone rang. A woman's voice said: "I bought a rectal thermometer in your store yesterday. There wasn't any instructions. What do I do with it?"

Mr. Donahue, next door, works on the railroad and often sleeps during the day, having just got off a freight drag to Kansas City or someplace. This makes it necessary for Rush and Vic to be quiet and curtails their activities at various times. There is no love in Vic and Rush for Donahue.

One day Mrs. Donahue was having company, including a small child, and Donahue needed to sleep, so Mrs. Donahue asked Sade if Donahue could flake out on the Gooks' couch in the living room. Sade said sure. When Rush comes home from school and sees the sleeping man, he declares, in mock seriousness, that Donahue looks dead. Sade tells him not to be silly. Vic comes home and Rush repeats the whimsy to his father:

JANUARY 28, 1935

RUSH: (*To Vic*) Too bad poor ol' Mr. Donahue hadda go an' die, wasn't it?

VIC: A great loss to us all. Say you gotta penny?

RUSH: Sure.

VIC: Produce it. I have a match.

RUSH: Here.

VIC: Fine. Now, betake yourself over by the book-case.

RUSH: (*Going*) Maybe we can grab Mr. Donahue right back from the angels.

VIC: We can only try. (***Strikes Match***)

RUSH: (***Off***) Let it go good an' hot.

VIC: Don't tell an old hand how to do this.

RUSH: Where ya gonna put it?

VIC: Between the knee an' the hip-bone that is known as the Children's Hour.

RUSH: Don't let it slide off.

VIC: I won't.

RUSH: All set?

VIC: (*Going Towards Rush*) Everything is in readiness.

RUSH: (*Up*) Maybe we oughta hide.

VIC: Oh, no.

RUSH: He might get mad.

VIC: Why? When he wakes up, he'll jump—an' when he jumps he'll knock the hot penny off his knee. There won't be the slightest evidence of our treachery.

RUSH: Heat oughta be workin' through his pants by this time.

VIC: It will, it will.

SADE: (*Returning*) That was the gas-meter man at the door. Whatcha doin' huddled over here by the wall?

VIC: You told us to keep quiet till you got back.

SADE: Oh. Well, like I started to say: why can't I lift up his legs an' slide the magazine out from under . . .

VIC: (***Impersonates Mr. Donahue: A Mighty Yell Of Fear***)

SADE: Heavens up above!

RUSH: He's alive, Mom. Mr. Donahue's alive!

END OF SCRIPT

ANNOUNCER: A rude awakening, Mr. Donahue . . . a rude awakening. And good listeners, with this rude awakening, we take leave of the small house half-way up in the next block for today.

Commercials And Closing

I went to the races Saturday with Frank Walsh and won $20. If I ever own a racehorse I am going to name him "Black Beauty." I think that is a fine name for a racehorse and it sure as hell will irritate everybody. I bet the announcer will grow white lipped and trembling as he announces that "Black Beauty" is doing thus and so. Another nice name for a racehorse, Harry? If I had two racehorses I would name them "Black Beauty" and "Victory." Frank Walsh is changing jobs. He leaves Sears Roebuck to work for an advertising agency.

Mr. Chinbunny, principal of Edwards School, visited the eighth grade this morning and said he hoped the graduating class would always keep a warm spot in their hearts for Edwards School and remember what it had done for them. When he left the room, Rooster Davis, who is always a whiz at "doping out ways to kill time and get outa studyin'—suggested to Miss Kinney that everybody make a list of the things they were gonna do for Edwards School when they got rich." Miss Kinney, who never can see through Rooster's tricks, said it was a a good idea, so they did it. Rush, who is Class Secretary, took charge of the lists when they were completed and brought them home to show his folks. Incidentally, the *Kitchenware Dealer's Quarterly* arrived this morning and Vic has been trying to read Sade a speech by R. W. Corbin. Sade wasn't interested and welcomed the interruption provided by Rush. Vic reads to himself, rather miffed.

RUSH: Well, here's Bulldog Drummond's good deeds. (*Reads*) I, Bulldog Drummond, when I get rich will do the following things: erect a statue of myself on the lawn facing Market Street. For this statue I will pay forty dollars.

SADE: That don't sound like much for a statue.

RUSH: Bulldog ain't used to big numbers. Lawrence Kirby though is different. Wait'll I read you his good deeds. He's gonna put a swimming-pool in Edwards School worth three million dollars.

SADE: Lands.

RUSH: Well, here's some more of Bulldog's: (*Reads*) I will place large pictures of myself in every room. I will plant flowers that spell out my name. I will change the name of Edwards School to Drummond School and have an electric sign out in front that says Drummond School.

SADE: Sounds like he's thinkin' more about himself than anything else.

RUSH: Yeah. That's Bulldog for ya. Blowin' about himself is one of his biggest characteristics.

SADE: Oh, he'll get over that when he gets older.

RUSH: Here's Mildred Tisdel's list. Wanta hear what she's gonna do?

SADE: Yes.

RUSH: I, Mildred Tisdel, hope some day to do the following things: Provide the primary grades with toys so the little children will like school at the very start. Improve the playground. Donate a library.

SADE: (*Approvingly*) Uh-huh.

RUSH: Here's Lawrence Kirby's. I, Lawrence Kirby, when I get rich will.

VIC: (*Explosive Laugh*)

SADE: Oh, goodness, Vic.

VIC: This R. W. Corbin oughta be put in jail, he's so funny.

SADE: Well, laugh to yourself.

VIC: Don't you wish you'd let me finish this speech out loud?

SADE: No. Go on, son.

RUSH: (*Reads*) I, Lawrence Kirby, when I get rich will do the following things: give five thousand dollars to Miss Kinney; five thousand dollars to Miss White; give five thousand dollars to Miss Jeffries; give five thousand dollars to Miss Taft; give five thousand . . . He's got all the Edwards School teachers down for that much money apiece, Mom.

SADE: He will hafta get rich.

RUSH: I'll say. Here's what Helen Keefer's gonna do: (*Reads*) I, Helen Keefer, when rich will do the following things: install candy cases on all floors. Give free music lessons to all pupils.

SADE: Uh-huh.

RUSH: Here's Hallie Wilson's. He couldn't think of anything. Here's Dorothy Ellis'. She couldn't think of anything either. Here's Mary Evans'. She copied off'n Lawrence Kirby's paper so she's got the same thing he's got only she upped him a thousand berries. (*Reads*) I, Mary Evan, when I get rich will do the following things: give six thousand dollars to Miss Kinney; give six thousand dollars to Miss White; give six thousand dollars to

	Miss Jeffries; give six thousand dollars to Miss Taft. An' so on.
SADE:	Uh-huh.
RUSH:	Here's mine.
SADE:	What you gonna do for Edwards School?
RUSH:	(*Reads*) I, Rush Gook, after getting rich will do the following things: tear down an' rebuild Edwards School at a cost of fourteen million dollars. Place solid gold roof on Edwards School at a cost of ten million dollars. Present every graduate with a diamond class pin at a cost of four million dollars. Install automatic drinking fountains in every room at a cost of three million dollars. Equip Edwards School athletic teams with special high-powered airplane at a cost of two million dollars. Give one million dollars to Miss Kinney; give one million dollars to Miss White; give one million dollars to Miss Jeffries; give one million dollars to Miss Taft.
SADE:	Gracious me!
RUSH:	Makes me out a pretty generous guy, don't it?
SADE:	I should say so. I wonder if there is that many million dollars in the whole . . .
VIC:	Hey, kiddo, how about dinner?
SADE:	Meat must be done by now. C'mon.
RUSH:	Oh say, Mom, before I forget.
SADE:	Yes?

RUSH: I . . . . I wonder if you could lend me five cents till Saturday.

END OF SCRIPT

ANNOUNCER: . . . which concludes a brief interlude at the small house half-way up in the next block. (*Pause*)

COMMERCIALS AND CLOSING

On June 4, Rush graduates from High School, and all three of our characters realize full well an important milestone has been reached. Rush promptly goes out and gets a job—at the Kitchenware Plant, in the boxing department. Vic is a little disturbed about this, but Rush assures him that he got the job strictly on his own merits and not because he's Vic's son. Vic gets used to the idea. It's pleasant, the two of them going down to work together in the morning, coming home for lunch together. Their comraderie now assumes a new quality. It's much more man to man. One day, on the lunch hour, Rush gets his Mom to come to the boxing department to see where he works. It's empty, all the workers having gone out to lunch.

RUSH SHOWS MOM BOXING DEPT.   AUGUST 8, 1935

RUSH: That bench in the corner is where Jack Speler works.

SADE: Is it?

RUSH: Yeah, an' the one in the other corner is Homer Greyman's.

SADE: (*Running Out Of Things To Say*) You really got quite a little place here.

RUSH: It is. Here.

SADE: What is it?

Rush: Brand new shiny six-penny nail. Take it home for a souvenir of your trip.

Sade: Thank you. I'll put it in my purse.

Rush: If ya wanta wait a minute, I'll take a hammer 'an smash two nails together into a little cross. Makes an attractive ornament to wear on your . . .

Sade: (*Hurriedly*) No, this'll do fine. This nail is just dandy.

Rush: O.K. Let's see now: what else is there to show you?

Sade: I've seen quite a bit, son, an' it's been fine. I . . .

Rush: Over there underneath the desk is the boss' old shoes.

Sade: Uh-huh.

Rush: Above the door we have a good-luck horse-shoe.

Sade: Uh-huh.

Rush: That black box is full of small tools for delicate work.

Sade: I see.

Rush: Right outside you can see a little furnace for burnin' trash.

Sade: Yes, sir.

Rush: The big cupboard contains our regular tools. Too bad I ain't got a key. Like to unlock it an' show you the different things.

SADE: Well, some other time you can . . .

RUSH: My work hat hangin' on the hook.

SADE: Uh-huh.

RUSH: An' Jack Speler's work hat right next to it.

SADE: Well.

RUSH: Homer Greyman's work hat on the other side.

SADE: Think of that.

RUSH: (**Looks Around**) Well, Mom, I . . . I guess that's all.

SADE: Better go, huh?

RUSH: Unless you can think of somethin' else I've mentioned around home ya wanta see.

SADE: No can't think of a thing.

RUSH: Shall we mosey on over to the Greek's then?

SADE: All right.

RUSH: Did ya get a kick outa this, Mom?

SADE: Oh—had a gorgeous time.

RUSH: Uh-huh. I imagine a woman enjoys visitin' the place where her kid holds down a job an' earns a classy salary.

END OF SCRIPT

ANNOUNCER: A woman does enjoy it, Rush. We did too. (*Pause*)

Closing and Commercial Credits

A dominant feature of Paul's personality was a distaste for sentiment. Sentiment made him laugh—and he could use it to make you laugh too. He had a great appreciation for real emotion, but for its mechanical sign-post he had only scorn. The obligatory attitudes that people assumed in the face of certain occurrences—sickness, death, misfortune, afflictions, were targets for his humor. Paul figured there was as much funniness in these circumstances as there was sadness and he rooted it out.

And he uses the phoney, repressive atmosphere created by people in the presence of something that is supposed to be solemn as the growth medium for humor, knowing that in this uneasy air laughs burst forth explosively, realizing that people know instinctively that this ponderous solemnity is a fraud, and that it needs only the slightest disturbance to send them into gales of laughter.

VIC AND SADE   (*Crisco*)   JULY 18, 1935   THURSDAY

THEY VISIT DONAHUE IN THE HOSPITAL

ANNOUNCER: OPENING AND COMMERCIAL CREDITS

INTRODUCTION: Our scene doesn't open in the small house half-way up in the next block today. Instead we take you to Wheeler Hospital, where Vic, Sade and young Rush have come to call on Mr. Donahue who was operated for appendicitis yesterday. And here on a bench in the main corridor are the gentlemen of the party waiting for Sade, who has gone to the office to inquire the whereabouts of Mr. Donahue's room. Listen.

VIC: Here, hold these doggone flowers a while.

RUSH: Mom told you to hold 'em. I'm liable to squish 'em.

VIC: You're big enough not to squish flowers.

RUSH: Yeah, but Mom insisted for you to hold 'em.

VIC: Thunder.

RUSH: Not heavy are they?

VIC: No, but I hate the smell of 'em.

RUSH: Hate the smell of Late Joe Butlers? Heck, I figure they got a pretty high-class smell.

VIC: They got a sickening smell.

RUSH: You prob'ly just smell this hospital smell.

VIC: Naw.

RUSH: It's a sickening smell. (*Laughs*)

VIC: What's the matter?

RUSH: I made an involuntary joke. I said the hospital had a sickening smell. Naturally it's got a sickening smell. It's full of sick people. (*Proceeds To Enjoy This Splendid Joke*)

VIC: (*Cutting Him Off*) Be still. Dontcha see all the signs around "Silence"?

RUSH: Aw, nobody heard me.

VIC: For all you know some poor sick guy down the hall heard that laughin', was afflicted with sudden shock, turned his face to the wall, an' quietly passed away.

RUSH: Aw. (*Chuckles*)

VIC: Funny, huh?

RUSH: No, but a little laughin' couldn't . . .

VIC: It might be best if we hold our tongue while in the hospital.

RUSH: Wonder what's keepin' Mom.

VIC: One doesn't know.

RUSH: There goes a fella with a bucket. He's got a white suit on just like . . .

SADE: (*Coming Up And Speaking In A Hissing Hospital Voice*) Boys.

VIC & RUSH: Yeah?

SADE: (*Up*) We're to go down this corridor to room 116. That's where Mr. Donahue is.

RUSH: Ain't any nurse going with us?

SADE: No, the lady at the desk said we could find the way by ourselves. C'mon, Vic.

VIC: I'm comin'.

SADE: (*A Dumb Question*) Got the flowers?

VIC: Whatcha s'pose these are?

SADE: Talk soft. This is a hospital, ya know.

VIC: Is it?

SADE: See all the signs around "Silence."

VIC: You take the flowers.

SADE: No. Look, the lady at the desk told me Mr. Donahue's asleep an' we mustn't disturb him. We can go in an' sit down but we gotta wait till he wakes up by himself.

VIC: Let's head for home then.

SADE: After comin' all the way out here?

VIC: What's the use sittin' around watchin' a guy sleep?

SADE: That's a fine way to talk about a poor fella that's had his insides all cut into. (**Raises Voice With All Due Hospital Limitations**) Rush, get away from there. What ya doin'?

RUSH: (*Off A Little*) Lookin' at the number on this door.

SADE: What is it?

RUSH: One-twelve.

SADE: We want one-sixteen.

RUSH: That oughta be the room at the end. Yeah, I believe it is.

SADE: C'mere by me. They don't want kids makin' a disturbance in the hall. (*To Vic*) Vic, the lady at the desk told me visitin' hours is over at seven o'clock. What time is it now?

VIC: Fifteen minutes till.

SADE: We only got a little bit to stay then. Let's talk cheerful to Mr. Donahue now, an' say he's lookin' just fine an' we bet he gets well so fast he . . . Rush,

	poke your shirt in your pants. Look like a bum. Is this the room?
RUSH:	Yea—one-sixteen.
SADE:	(*Low Tones*) I'll peek in first an' see if . . .
VIC:	Take these flowers, Rush.
SADE:	Keep the flowers. I'll peek in first an' . . . Where's the door-knob here?
RUSH:	It's a swingin' door, Mom. All hospital doors are . . .
SADE:	Oh, uh-huh. C'mon boys—follow me in very very softly. We don't wanta wake him up an' . . .
RUSH:	(*Suddenly*) Ouch!
SADE:	(*In Hissing Infuriation*) What ails you, sir?
RUSH:	Gov kicked me in the ankle.
VIC:	I didn't mean to kick ya. I had these doggone flowers up in front of my face an' couldn't see where the heck I was . . .
SADE:	Be still. We got a sick man in here.
RUSH:	(*Cheerfully*) By gosh there's Mr. Donahue in the bed, O.K. Sound asleep. I expect the terrible pain has . . .
SADE:	Don't let that door slam.
RUSH:	It can't slam. It's a swinging door. All hospital doors . . .
SADE:	Come over here by me.

VIC: Here's the flowers, Sade.

SADE: Huh?

VIC: Here's the flowers.

SADE: I don't want the flowers. Say, he looks wasted, don't he?

VIC: Yeah. Rush, take these doggone flowers before I . . .

SADE: You keep them flowers. Yes, sir, he does look wasted. Funniest thing: a person can be feelin' fine as a cucumber one minute an' the next minute they been operated on for appendicitis an' lose six pounds. Did I tell you Mr. Donahue lost six pounds?

VIC: Did they weight him?

SADE: I s'pose so. How else could they tell?

VIC: One way is to slice a banana into thin even cubes, rub fish in the hair, an' add up the number of vice-presidents of all the tin manufacturing companies in Northern . . .

SADE: Lower your voice if ya wanta talk. The lady at the desk told me not to interfere with him till he woke up of his own accord. Rush, what you gonna do?

RUSH: Sit down in this chair.

SADE: Well, don't rock.

RUSH: It's not a rockin' chair.

SADE: (*To Vic*) He looks as natural as can be, don't he?

VIC:	Why shouldn't he? He's not dead.
SADE:	(*Sharply*) Who said he was dead?
VIC:	That's the way ya talk about people in coffins . . . "By gosh, Mr. Dunkley looks as natural as Adam."
SADE:	(***Exasperation And Reproach***) Vic, this poor fella had a very serious operation yesterday morning—a very serious operation.
VIC:	Uh-huh.
SADE:	It don't pay to make jokes about things like that.
VIC:	I wasn't makin' any doggone jokes.
SADE:	(***Looking At Donahue Again***) Yes, sir, you can tell by his face what he's been through. Poor ol' Mr. Donahue; always so pleasant to everybody. Took down terrible sick without a smidgin of warning. Might happen to any of us. Just the day before yesterday Mis' Gooley there on East Street told about her cousin in Milwaukee gettin' kicked by a horse. He was walkin' down town without a worry in the world an' this horse . . . Look: believe he's gonna wake up.
VIC:	(***Impersonating Mr. Donahue—Produces Sleepy Grunts And Grumbles***)
SADE:	Yes, sir, believe he's gonna wake up. (*Lifts Voice*) Rush, he's gonna wake up.
RUSH:	(*Cooly*) That so?
SADE:	Stand back from the bed, Vic.

VIC: I'm not gonna hurt him.

SADE: Stand back from the bed. I believe he's gonna . . .

VIC: (*Mr. Donahue—Snorts, Grunts, Moans And Gives A Little Whistle That Dies*)

SADE: Oh, poor fella. Sufferin' in his sleep.

VIC: Aw. (*A Rather Loud Chuckle*)

SADE: Stop that!

VIC: Guys don't suffer in their sleep. Guys suffer when they're awake.

SADE: Well, don't you let you any more loud laughings.

RUSH: (*With Interest*) He open his eyes?

SADE: No, he turned over a little is all. What you got in your mouth?

RUSH: Carmel.

SADE: Where'd you get it?

RUSH: Whole box of 'em here on the table.

SADE: You actually touched poor Mr. Donahue's carmels somebody give him?

RUSH: There's about a bushel of 'em.

SADE: You put that back, sir.

RUSH: I got it half swallowed.

SADE: Did you hear that, Vic? He helped himself to candy.

VIC: (*Interested*) Where is the candy?

SADE: You just dare touch that box.

RUSH: It's carmels, Gov. You don't like carmels.

VIC: Heck, why don't he have some decent candy around? I could stand a hunk of milk chocolate.

SADE: (*Mad*) I bet I take you two to the hospital the next time somebody gets operated on.

VIC: Wouldn't hurt my feelin's to get left home. Somehow hospitals ain't my idea of fun.

SADE: We didn't come here to have fun.

VIC: What did we come here for . . . to watch Donahue sleep?

SADE: I'd be ashamed, Vic.

VIC: It's almost seven o'clock. When that bell rings we got to beat it. If he don't wake up pretty quick this trip'll be all for nothin'.

SADE: I think he's wakin' up now. Stand back from the bed. Give him a chance.

VIC: I don't see what my standin' away from the bed has got to do with . . .

SADE: Don't talk.

VIC: (*Mr. Donahue—Produces A Number Of Surprising*

Noises, Terminating In Sleepy Ones That Fade Away And Stop)

SADE: (*All Heart And Sympathy*) Poor fella.

VIC: Sounds all right to me.

RUSH: (*Off A Little*) He wake up?

SADE: No. You eatin' more of them carmels?

RUSH: This is the same carmel I had before. Tough baby.

VIC: Wish to thunder I could sit down.

SADE: Well, sit down.

VIC: Where? Pete's got the only chair.

SADE: It won't hurt you to stand up a minute while you're callin' on a neighbor that's had his appendix out.

VIC: These flowers are drivin' me crazy.

SADE: Oh—flowers drivin' you crazy.

VIC: I can't stand the smell of Late Joe Butler flowers.

SADE: Goodness, such a fella. Here, give me the . . . No, hold 'em a minute. I'll see if there's room for 'em with the roses here in the bowl.

RUSH: Mom.

SADE: What?

RUSH: That bell's gonna ring pretty quick an' we'll hafta go. Let's wake Mr. Donahue up.

SADE:	Don't talk foolish.
RUSH:	He'll never know we called on him.
SADE:	The lady at the desk'll tell him he had visitors.
RUSH:	Whatcha say I give a couple coughs?
SADE:	Coughs?
RUSH:	Sure—snap him out of it. Like this: (*Coughs Stranglingly*)
SADE:	(*Horrified*) Rush, stop that this minute.
RUSH:	I only wanted to . . .
SADE:	The idea!
VIC:	Is there a place for these flowers on the dresser?
SADE:	No, the bowl is crowded as it is.
VIC:	(*Mean Anguish*)
SADE:	What's the matter?
VIC:	I got to stand up an' I gotta hold flowers.
SADE:	Oh, my, a person'd think you was little china doll or somethin'. Seems like a great big man could . . . (*Giggles*) Hey, here's a little card he got from somebody. Listen: "The doctor may butcher; the doctor may hack. But when you catch him in heaven you can break his darn back."
VIC:	That musta cheered up the invalid. In fact (*Hospital Bell Rings*)

RUSH: There's the bell, Mom.

SADE: I heard it. C'mon, boys.

VIC: Heck, we come all the way out here an' waste a whole evening an' . . .

SADE: You two go ahead. An' tip-toe.

RUSH: I got shoes that's hard to tip-toe in. My feet kinda bend around an' hurt like . . .

SADE: (*Off A Little*) An' don't talk.

RUSH: (*Low Tones To Vic*) Have a carmel, Gov. They're not bad. Got a chocolat-y flavor.

VIC: (*Low Tones*) O.K. I'll try one.

RUSH: Take two. I swiped half a dozen.

VIC: Thanks.

SADE: (*Coming Up*) I adjusted his covers good around his shoulders. Ready to go?

VIC & RUSH: Sure.

SADE: Move along then. (*To The Sleeper*) Good-bye, Mr. Donahue, get well real quick. (*To Her Family Briskly*) C'mon fellas.

VIC: Sade.

SADE: Yes?

VIC: Will you carry the flowers home?

END OF SCRIPT

ANNOUNCER: And so we've spent a little while in Wheeler Hospital at bedside of Mr. Donahue . . . in company with our friends who live in the small house half-way up in the next block. (*Pause*)

CLOSING AND COMMERCIAL CREDITS

Little boys that's blunt and saucy, little boys that's sharp and bossy, never upon the President's chair will squat, but in a prison cell will rot.

I have invented a bicycle that works on the principle of the typewriter and I have invented a physic that works on the Principal of the High School.

Gee, I guess this isn't much of a letter.

I miss you, Harry, and wish we could take a ride together on Saturday.

'Voir

Paul Mills Rhymer
(Goodlooking, talented, rich and popular)

WALTER B. PANTLY   NOVEMBER 12, 1935

VIC: A very remarkable man. He had both his legs cut off by a train when he was forty-two years old an' when he was sixty-two he was able to roller skate.

RUSH: How could he do that?

VIC: By practicing constantly. His chief claim to fame, however, was his discovery of the second flavor in peanuts.

Rush: Second flavor in peanuts?

Vic: Yeah. There's two flavors in peanuts.

Rush: I only know of one.

Vic: Look: you've eaten a batch of peanuts.

Rush: O.K.

Vic: When you first began on the peanuts they had one flavor.

Rush: Yeah?

Vic: After you've got down a whole sack full they taste a little different. Ain't that right?

Rush: Why . . . a . . . Yes, I guess it is.

Vic: The discovery of Walter B. Pantly.

Rush: I don't see how you can call it a discovery.

Vic: I don't see why I can't call it a discovery.

Rush: Everybody knows that about peanuts.

Vic: Yes, but who, besides Walter B. Pantly, had the courage of his convictions an' get his discovery registered at the Capitol building in Washington D.C.?

Rush: He do all that?

Vic: He did all that. Broken in body an' sick in spirit as he was. Now when you go to Washington D.C. you notice great crowds standin' in front of a metal tablet, sacred to the memory of Walter B. Pantly, discoverer of the second flavor in peanuts. Have another piece of steak?

Here's one of those one-sided phone conversations I mentioned earlier. The situation is that Mildred Tisdell broke off a tooth this morning playing basketball at school . . .

MILDRED LOSES A TOOTH   NOVEMBER 18, 1935

RUSH: (*To Phone*) 2572-X, please. Correct. (*Chuckles To Himself*)

VIC: What's funny, George?

RUSH: This is gonna be rich.

SADE: (*Tough*) What's gonna be rich?

RUSH: Mildred lisps.

SADE: She what?

RUSH: She lisps. Rooster just told me. She goes . . . (*Mocks Mildred*) Thith ith the day we go thwimming. Thith ith a thwell thtocking. Leth play horth. Thith ith . . .

SADE: (*Tough*) Rush Gook, you hang up that receiver. Hang it up, I say. That poor little miserable . . .

RUSH: (*To Phone*) Hello, Mildred? Rush, Mildred. Say, I just heard the bad news. Milton Welch told me. I'm certainly sorry you . . . Huh? Huh? What? (*Laughs*) What?

SADE: Rush.

RUSH: Hold the wire one second, Mildred. (*To Sade*) Whatcha say, Mom?

SADE: What a nasty thing to do. Laugh at a poor little kid that . . .

RUSH: I wasn't laughin' at her. Only she talks so funny with that tooth out I can't help . . .

SADE: Hang up that receiver like I told you.

RUSH: I hafta tell her good-bye, don't I?

SADE: Tell her good-bye then.

RUSH: (*To Phone*) Hello, Mildred? Say, I won't keep you; I just called to express my sympathy. Yeah. So I'll . . . Huh? Huh? What? (*Laughs*) Whatcha say? (*Laughs*) Huh?

SADE: (*Tough*) Rush.

RUSH: (*Trying To Stop Laughing*) Just a minute, Mom. (*To Phone*) Mildred, I couldn't quite make out what you . . . Huh? Oh, tellin' me how it happened, huh? I see. Yeah. Yeah . . . (*Low Tone To Gov*) C'mere, Gov.

VIC: What for?

RUSH: I wanta hold the receiver to your ear.

VIC: Why?

RUSH: Mildred's tellin' how she knocked her tooth out. Listen to her once. (*Mocks Mildred*) Hist hast wisht testhed bunch kosh . . .

VIC:	Put your hand over the mouth-piece.
RUSH:	I got it against my chest. She can't hear.
SADE:	That's a rotten mean trick.
RUSH:	Aw, Mom, it don't hurt to . . . Hear her, Gov?
VIC:	Holy smoke.
RUSH:	Ain't that rich?
VIC:	She sounds like she was talkin' from the bottom of the bath-tub c'mere, Sade.
SADE:	I will not.
VIC:	C'mere.
RUSH:	Let me listen again, Gov.
VIC:	Go 'way. (*Listening*) Never heard such a doggone lingo.
RUSH:	It's my turn to listen.
VIC:	She sounds like she had a quart of axle grease in her mouth an' was tryin' to . . . Listen once, Sade.
SADE:	(***Who, After All, Is Curious***) Move over then.
RUSH:	It's my turn.
SADE:	Move over.
VIC:	(*To Rush*) Keep that mouth-piece covered up, Pete, so she don't . . .

SADE:	(*Astonished*) My lands.
VIC:	Did you ever in your life . . .
SADE:	She must have had nine teeth knocked out. Oh, the poor little miserable . . . Rush, she's stopped talkin'. Say something.
RUSH:	Gimme the receiver then.
SADE:	Here, take it.
RUSH:	(*To Phone*) So that's how it happened, huh, Mildred? Well, it sure was tough. I'm sorry as heck. Huh? Huh? What? Whatcha say? Oh—"Hafta hang up now"? O.K., Mildred, I won't keep you any longer. Huh? What? What? Oh—"good-bye"? Good-bye, Mildred. (*Hangs Up*)
SADE:	Oh, I could just cry.
VIC:	The little tyke is in bad shape.
RUSH:	(*Pleasurably*) Doggone.
VIC:	What's eatin' you?
RUSH:	Nothing' at all. I was just thinkin' how situations change. Ten minutes ago I thought life was dull. All of a sudden it picked up. Diversion fell right in my lap. (*Chuckles*) I guess it's a jolly life.

END OF SCRIPT

ANNOUNCER:	Which concludes another brief interlude at the small house half-way up in the next block. (*Pause*)

CLOSING AND COMMERCIAL CREDITS

A lady was in a zoo and she saw two porcupines and she said to the zookeeper 'is there any difference between those two porcupines?' and he said 'yes, one of them has a longer prick than the other' and the lady was insulted and went to the curator's office and said 'I am insulted' and told him about what the smart-aleck zookeeper had said and the curator laughed and said the zookeeper never meant any harm, he meant 'quill' when he said prick. And then he added in kindly tones, 'The pricks are the same.'

I had my picture in TIME MAGAZINE. I bet you never had your picture in TIME MAGAZINE.

We got self-operating elevators in our building now.

Did you ever manage to overcome the masturbation habit? Wire me yes or no.

NOVEMBER 20, 1935

SADE: Vic, it was Mis' Grooderman that told me this an' she's got the name of bein' a terrible gossip an' busybody. Even if she is a terrible gossip an' busybody there's no doubt what she told me is true.

VIC: What'd she tell ya?

SADE: She told me what Mis' Kneesuffer said about Rush.

VIC: What'd she say about him?

SADE: All kinds of mean things. I couldn't hardly believe it. Here all along I been thinkin' she was such a fine friend. Axle grease wouldn't melt in her mouth she's so sweet an' mealy. An' all the time she goes around runnin' down a person's children. Rush, stand up so I can see your head.

RUSH: My head?

SADE: Yes. Stand up.

RUSH: (*Astonished*) Can't ya see my head now? I'm sittin' right here. If ya can't even see my head, them glasses you got must be cast-iron . . .

SADE: Don't be smarty. I wanta see the shape of your head. Vic, has he got a funny-shaped head?

VIC: Yeah. His head is just like . . .

SADE: Can you imagine Mis' Kneesuffer that lets on to be so sweet goin' around tellin' people somebody else's kids got funny-shaped heads? Turn around once, son. Let's see the back.

RUSH: Back of my head?

VIC: Kiddo, he has got kind of a funny-shaped head.

SADE: (***The Mother With Her Chick***) He has not.

VIC: It's just exactly like . . .

SADE: That head looks all right to me. I see nothing wrong with that head.

VIC: There's nothing wrong with it. I was only sayin' . . .

SADE: You started to say it was just exactly like something. What is it just exactly like?

VIC: It's just exactly like my head.

SADE: Have you got a funny-lookin' head?

VIC:		Sure. You know how hard it is for me to get a hat that fits.
SADE:		You have an unusual head. You an' Rush both got unusual heads.
VIC:		That's what I say. Our heads are kinda rounded out an' . . .
SADE:		"Unusual" is different from "funny."
VIC:		Well, maybe so, but . . .
SADE:		Rush has a handsome head.
VIC:		O.K. That's a compliment for both of us. Don't forget though that before we were married you yourself used to kid me about my head. Called me "Punkin" there for a while.
SADE:		That's altogether different. That's altogether different. What I'm talkin' about is Mis' Kneesuffer.
VIC:		Did she say . . .
SADE:		It's not that I'm stickin' up for Mis' Grooderman's gossip or anything like that. But as long as she did tell me what Mis' Kneesuffer said, I stood there in Yamilton's an' drank it all in. An' it just makes me mad as hops. (*Scornfully*) "Funny-lookin' head." I'd like to know how she can talk about people. That brother of hers—that Tubby—so fat he can't hardly waddle along.
VIC:		He can't help that.
SADE:		You stickin' up for Mis' Kneesuffer?

VIC: No, I'm stickin' up for Tubby. He's not a bad . . .

SADE: What was that business he got himself into there in Chicago? Had to go to court or some place?

VIC: He was a witness in a street car accident.

SADE: Uh-huh, there you are. Let Mis' Kneesuffer keep her own brothers outa jail before she jumps on anybody else. "Funny-lookin' head." (*Tenderly To Rush*) Don't you care one bit, son.

RUSH: (*Chuckling*) I don't. I'm satisfied with my head. It's a little rounder than most people's but . . .

SADE: Next time you see Mis' Kneesuffer you be just as nice as pie to her. That's the way.

RUSH: I don't hold any grudge. Hundreds of people have passed the remark that my head . . .

SADE: No sir, Vic, if I was Mis' Kneesuffer I wouldn't open my mouth about anybody else. That Tubby. Don't see anything so wonderful about his head.

VIC: He's a college graduate an' a registered pharmacist.

SADE: I'll say he is, the big ol' fatty. Ya know what I could of done this afternoon?

VIC: What?

SADE: I could of said some mean things to Mis' Grooderman about Mis' Kneesuffer. Bein' such a monstrous gossip she'd run straight to her fast as she could. But I wouldn't lower myself.

VIC: No.

SADE: No, sir, I wouldn't lower myself. (*Bitterly*) "Funny-lookin' head." (*To Rush*) Your head's all right, sonny. Don't let what any ol' person says about it bother you.

RUSH: I don't. I take my head as it comes. I realize . . .

SADE: Anybody says anything smart to you, just send 'em around to your mother.

RUSH: O.K.

SADE: Tonight we're gonna have mince pie an' thin round steak like you like.

RUSH: Fine.

SADE: An' chocolate milk.

RUSH: Dandy.

SADE: I guess I might as well go get things started. Getting late.

VIC: Rodney, do you wish to continue . . .

SADE: (*Moving Off*) Vic, I'm gonna need groceries. Wanta stroll over to the store?

VIC: You talkin' to me?

SADE: (*Off A Little*) Yes.

VIC: I thought grocery-getting was in Rush's department.

SADE: (*Further Off*) Wouldn't hurt you to go once in a while.

VIC: (*To Rush*) Well, I'll be darned.

RUSH: (*Chuckling*) Mom thinks my feelin's is hurt.

VIC: Yeah.

RUSH: She's the one with the hurt feelin's.

VIC: Yeah. Mother stuff.

RUSH: Huh?

VIC: Mothers with kids are like hens with chicks. Touch my chick an' by gosh I'll peck your leg off. Say anything about my son's head an' by gosh I'll never speak to you again.

RUSH: (*Chuckles*) Sure.

VIC: As a matter of fact, you have got a funny lookin' head.

RUSH: I know it.

VIC: Well, ya wanta finish this game?

RUSH: Yeah.

VIC: Move.

END OF SCRIPT

Chapter Nine — 1936

Vic And Sade   (*Crisco*)

Sade & Ruthie Have A Fight   January 3, 1936   Friday

Announcer: Opening And Commercial Credits

Introduction: Well sir, it's a few minutes or so past eleven o'clock in the morning as our scene opens now, and here in the kitchen of the small house half-way up in the next block we discover Mrs. Victor Gook industriously bending over her ironing-board. Tuesday is the time usually given over to this task, but the holidays have more or less thrown Sade off schedule. And so she irons. But there's a newcomer approaching apparently . . . because the back door is opening. Listen.

Sade: (*As Door Opens*) Grocery boy?

Vic: (*Off A Little*) Husband boy.

Sade: Oh, h'lo there.

Vic: I'll say. Still at it?

Sade: (*As Door Closes*) Still at it.

Vic: (*Drawing Closer*) Colder'n Billy Jackson out-doors.

SADE: You home for dinner already?

VIC: Nope. Just steppin' in for one second. The boss is waitin' for me out in front.

SADE: Oh, is he?

VIC: We're on our way to the court-house to file some papers. I left my brief-case home this morning. Some dope in it we hafta have.

SADE: Yes, I noticed you left it. I put it in the library table swing-back.

VIC: (*Moving Off*) O.K. I'll trot in an' . . .

SADE: Wait a second, will ya?

VIC: Huh?

SADE: Vic, I . . . I think I'll call Ruthie after all.

VIC: (*Back Again*) Thought you'd done that.

SADE: No.

VIC: You said you were going to.

SADE: Yes, but I told you I'd changed my mind.

VIC: When I talked to you on the phone at nine-thirty you said you'd changed your mind back again.

SADE: I changed it back again again.

VIC: Aw, for gosh sakes.

SADE: Well, what's a person to do? It was all Ruthie's

	fault. She started the squabble. It's her place to phone.
VIC:	Wait till she does phone then.
SADE:	But she hasn't phoned.
VIC:	(*Moving Off*) Well, you work it out for yourself . . . I hafta . . .
SADE:	Wait, Vic.
VIC:	Mr. Ruebush is sittin' out in the car. I can't keep him all day.
SADE:	Will you phone Ruthie for me?
VIC:	Why?
SADE:	Because . . . Well, here's the way it is, Vic—Ruthie knows that fight was all her fault. An' I bet she's just cryin' herself sick over there. But she can't bring herself to call up because . . . Well, you know how a person is. They hate to admit they're in the wrong. I'd be the same way myself if I was her.
VIC:	Well?
SADE:	An' I hesitate from callin' her up because . . . well, because I'm the injured party, don'tcha see? It's not my bee's-wax to be phonin' somebody that was mean to me.
VIC:	Tell ya what ya do: figure it all out an' decide what's best an' this noon when I come home you can . . .
SADE:	Will you phone her?

VIC: I got nothin' to say to her.

SADE: No, but once you get her on the wire it'd give her a chance to ask if Sade is there.

VIC: An' then what?

SADE: An' then she could do her apologizin' to me.

VIC: What if she don't feel like apologizin'?

SADE: That's what I mean. Don'tcha see? If I phoned an' she didn't feel like apologizin' I'd look like a ninny.

VIC: (*Moving Off*) O.K. I'll take care of it this noon.

SADE: Why don'tcha do it now?

VIC: Because Mr. Ruebush is out by the curb freezin' his whiskers off.

SADE: Only take you half a second.

VIC: Kiddo, we're on our way to the court-house. I can't stall around here.

SADE: No, but think of poor Ruthie. She's had time to think things over an' I just bet she feels awful. I bet she's strainin' her ears listenin' for the phone bell to ring. (*Pleading*) C'mon.

VIC: (*Giving In*) What's the number—2572-x?

SADE: 2572-x.

VIC: I hope the boss don't . . . Hey, what'll I say to Ruthie when she answers?

SADE: Say . . . "This is Vic."

VIC: "This is Vic?"

SADE: Sure.

VIC: A very interesting telephone message. I'll ring her up an' say "This is Vic." After that thrilling statement I'll say good-bye, huh?

SADE: Tell her . . . Ask her . . . Ask her if she got . . . if she got your Christmas card all right.

VIC: I never sent her any Christmas card.

SADE: I did.

VIC: O.K. I'll say: "This is Vic. Did you get Sade's Christmas card all right?"

SADE: For heaven's sake, don't mention my name.

VIC: Kiddo, please. I got to get going.

SADE: Well, call.

VIC: Tell me what to say.

SADE: Say . . . Oh, I don't know.

VIC: Look: you decide just how you want the matter handled an' when I come home for dinner I'll . . .

SADE: No. Poor Ruthie over there sobbin' her heart out.

VIC: I'll ask her if Fred's home. How's that?

SADE: Yeah. Yeah, ask her if Fred's home.

VIC: 2472-x?

SADE: 2472-x?

VIC: (*Lifting Receiver*) Hope poor ol' Mr. Ruebush don't die out there in the terrible sub-zero . . . (*To Phone*) 2472-x, please. Correct (*To Sade*) . . . in the terrible sub-zero . . .

SADE: (*Quickly*) Hang up, Vic.

VIC: Huh?

SADE: Hang up.

VIC: What in the name of . . .

SADE: Hang up I say.

VIC: (*Hanging Up*) Sade, this is . . .

SADE: She answer?

VIC: She never had time to answer. The operator didn't get through pluggin' in . . .

SADE: I decided it's better not to phone her after all. It's not my place to do the patchin'. She insulted me when I was a guest in her house. I'm the one with the dirty end of the stick an' she's the one that's got to make the first move. Don't you think so?

VIC: Sure.

SADE: If she's cryin' her head off an' mad at herself it's no look-out of mine. What I really ought to do is . . . Where ya doin'?

VIC:	(*Moving Off*) In an' get my brief-case an beat it.
SADE:	Wait.
VIC:	No, doggone it. I've had enough of this . . .
SADE:	I don't want you to phone again. Listen, how'd it be if I sent Rush over there this noon with . . . (*Phone: Excited*) There she is. There she is, Vic.
VIC:	Swell. Expect me home for dinner about . . .
SADE:	You gotta answer it.
VIC:	Me?
SADE:	Yes. An' listen . . . (*Phone Again*) Don't answer it yet. Don't answer it yet. Look: I'll pretend I'm outa the kitchen. I'll pretend I'm upstairs.
VIC:	Why?
SADE:	I don't want her to think I'm hangin' around waitin' for the phone to ring.
VIC:	Oh, shucks.
SADE:	Well, I don't. She's been mean to me an' I'd just as soon she thought I let it all roll off a duck's back. (*Phone*)
VIC:	Women are just plain hay-wire.
SADE:	Why dontcha answer that?
VIC:	You said you were going upstairs.
SADE:	I'm just pretending I'm upstairs.

VIC: Shall I pick up the receiver?

SADE: No. Yes, I mean.

VIC: What do you mean? Yes or no. (*Phone Again*)

SADE: No. Yes.

VIC: Yes?

SADE: Yes.

VIC: (*To Phone*) Hello? Yes. Why . . . a . . . I believe so. Believe she's upstairs. Just a second. (*Ordinary Tones*) Sade, you're wanted on the . . .

SADE: (*Hissing*) Holler.

VIC: Huh?

SADE: (*Hissing*) Put your hand over that transmitter.

VIC: It's covered. Whatcha mean "holler"?

SADE: If I'm upstairs you got to holler loud so I can hear you.

VIC: Oh.

SADE: Now take your hand off the thing.

VIC: O.K.

SADE: (*Hissing*) Holler.

VIC: (*Hollers*) Sade. Oh, Sade. Come on down from upstairs. You're wanted on the phone. (*To Phone*) Hold the wire just a moment.

SADE:	(*Low Tones*) How's she sound?
VIC:	O.K.
SADE:	Got your hand over the transmitter business?
VIC:	Yeah.
SADE:	Does she sound like she's sorry?
VIC:	Yeah.
SADE:	How'd I better answer?
VIC:	"Hello."
SADE:	I mean . . . hadn't I better say "Yes" real bright till I find out it's Ruthie an' then change my voice a little?
VIC:	Good idea.
SADE:	I'll say, (*Brightly*) "Yes?" An' then, (*Politely Inquiring*) "Oh, yes, Mis' Stembottom?"
VIC:	Great stuff. Here, take the receiver. You've had time to get downstairs.
SADE:	No, It'd look like I ran.
VIC:	Kiddo, I can't let my boss freeze to death out there at the curb.
SADE:	(*Who Is Upset To Begin With*) Oh, forget your boss five seconds.
VIC:	(*Tough*) Forget him! I s'pose you'd have me put this silly nonsense ahead of business. I s'pose you'd . . .

SADE: Don't aggravate me, Vic. Got enough on my mind already.

VIC: As though I got nothin' on my mind. Holy smokes, I . . .

SADE: Now give me that phone.

VIC: Take it.

SADE: Stick around a minute.

VIC: I can't stick around a . . .

SADE: (*To Vic*) Hush. (*To Phone—In Her Sweetest Tones*) Mis' Gook speakin'. What? Who is this? Oh. Oh. No, he hasn't. No. No, he hasn't showed up yet. Perfectly all right. Good-bye. (*Hangs Up: Raiser Voice To Call Bitterly To Her Husband*) Vic, c'mere.

VIC: (*Off A Little*) Kiddo, I got to get my briefcase an' . . .

SADE: C'mere, I said.

VIC: (*Returning*) What the heck's wrong now?

SADE: Why didn't you tell me that wasn't Ruthie?

VIC: I didn't know it wasn't Ruthie.

SADE: It was Mis' Croucher at the grocery store.

VIC: What'd she want?

SADE: Wanted to speak with the grocery boy if he was here. (*Mad*) Such a lot of craziness I never seen before in my life.

VIC:	I always did think Mother Croucher was little bats. She . . .
SADE:	I'm talking' about you.
VIC:	Me? What on earth have I done?
SADE:	All that stuff about pretendin' I was upstairs.
VIC:	That was your idea.
SADE:	You should of found out if it was Ruthie on the phone or not.
VIC:	(*Moving Off*) O.K. O.K. It's all my fault. I know I'm to blame for . . .
SADE:	C'mere.
VIC:	Huh?
SADE:	I'm tired of these monkey-shines. If Ruthie Stembottom ain't got the courage to call up an' admit she's wrong I'm not gonna be small about it. Telephone her.
VIC:	Sade, Mr. Ruebush is out there in the bitter cold prob'ly writin' my discharge papers this very moment. I can't . . .
SADE:	Let's get this over with.
VIC:	You don't want me to lose my . . .
SADE:	Number is 2572-x.
VIC:	What'll I say to her?

SADE:	Don't care what you say to her.
VIC:	This is Vic?
SADE:	Huh?
VIC:	(*Stupidly*) This is Vic.
SADE:	Oh, goodness, baby-talk—now of all times.
VIC:	Shall I say "This is Vic?" to Ruthie?
SADE:	Yes.
VIC:	If I ever get mixed up in any half-wit didoes like this again you can . . . (*Phone*)
SADE:	There she is. There she is.
VIC:	Want me to answer?
SADE:	Of course. Of course. Remember—I'm upstairs now.
VIC:	(*Stupidly*) You're upstairs?
SADE:	Yes. Like we done before. (*Phone*)
VIC:	Shall I say . . .
SADE:	Say that Sade is upstairs is all ya hafta say.
VIC:	An' to hold the line a minute, huh?
SADE:	Sure. (*Phone*)
VIC:	Shall I . . .

SADE: Answer it, Vic. She's liable to think I'm not home.

VIC: (*To Phone*) Yes? Oh, hello there. One second. (*To Sade*) Sade.

SADE: (*Hissing*) Holler.

VIC: (*Hollers*) Oh, Sade. You're wanted on the phone.

SADE: Now give me plenty of time to get down.

VIC: This is Rush on the . . .

SADE: Cover up that transmitter with your . . . Who?

VIC: Rush.

SADE: On the phone?

VIC: Yeah.

SADE: (*Irritated No End*) Oh, my heavens' sake's alive!

VIC: Well, you told me to holler. Thunder, I can't . . .

SADE: Gimme that. An' you stick around.

VIC: I got to go see if Mr. Ruebush is . . .

SADE: Stick around because you got to call up Ruthie for me. (*To Phone*) Yes, Rush. What? Eat at the cafeteria this noon? Got money? When'll ya be home? Uh-huh—well, don't bring any boys with ya because there's errands to be run. Yes. All right. What? Where was I that Gov had to holler. Oh, nowhere. No. You run on an' eat with your friends. Huh? Look, son, I hafta hang up now because I wanta use the phone for another call.

Yes. Eat a nice hot dinner now. All right. Good-bye. (*Hangs Up*; *To Vic*) He's gonna take lunch at the Greek's with . . . Vic. Where are ya? (*Calls*) Vic. (*Pause*) Oh, Vic. Vic. (*Pause*) (*And Then Hotly To Herself*) Sneaked out on me.

End of Script

ANNOUNCER: Sade, being absolutely honest with you we don't know as we blame him. (*Pause*)

Closing and Commercial Credits

At this time there was a young lady working in one of the offices and her name was Morgan Perron. Morgan was a short, solid, squarish young lady whose hobby was mountain climbing. She was jolly, good-natured, like "one of the boys." Laughed easily, and thought Paul was the funniest man alive. Paul was always quick to respond to anyone who had this estimate of him, and a warm, kidding relationship developed between them. His first expression of affection was to write to a bunch of mail-order houses that dealt in odd items, like "Little Miracle" trusses, bedpans, pills to restore lost vigor, manure spreaders, toilet deodorizers, etc. and enclose Morgan's name and address. Her desk was piled high for days with brochures, letters and samples, and her reaction was explosive. The story of the fine joke spread around NBC fast.

A little while later Paul began sending her postcards. Morgan was the first recipient of Paul's "funny post-cards." The success of these first cards, which were shown all over NBC and throughout a large portion of Chicago, encouraged Paul to continue the practice until his death. Those people he marked for special favors received post-cards. All his close friends have collections of them. I received them almost daily during the years I was in the Navy, and, when I left one base in Texas, the mailman had scribbled on the bottom of the last one, "I'm going to miss these."

He went to some pains with the post-cards. Many of them were vintage cards he bought at junk stores along Clark and State Streets in Chicago. Some bore pictures of old silent screen stars, some had pictures of strange people whom no one had ever heard of. Some had scenes of old towns, and most had an awkward, graceless, bad taste feeling about them—"Camp" for that day. But Paul was often not satisfied with the pictures displayed, and would doctor them in some way, sometimes pasting his own face on the bathing-suited body of some ancient charmer, or pasting an entirely different picture over the one furnished on the card.

Of course with his constant desire to explore all angles he developed refinements and innovations. As his pal Frank Walsh recalls:

"In this game much information and innuendo that should have been confined to private correspondence was scrawled on the backs of postal cards and mailed off—usually to the wives and daughters, presumably the more shockable members of the family. More than once in the early stages of the game Paul would inscribe some 'naughty' or slightly salacious message to my wife, then deliberately misdirect the card to an address elsewhere on the block or across the street. Getting these messages after close perusal by the neighbors could represent a new high in embarrassment.

"But one of his funniest moves was to address any number of complimentary messages to himself: 'Paul Rhymer, World's Greatest Radio Writer,' and deliberately misdirect the cards to the public relations department at CBS, the rival network. After much handling and reading by professional colleagues all along the line these messages would find their way back to NBC. More than once the ingrown messages were hand delivered by Charlie Lyon, the old pal and announcer who had assignments at both networks. When Charlie would hand over the card scrawled in Paul's own writing with flowery tributes to Rhymer's radio writing skill, the contretemps would fracture both of them. Me too, in retrospect."

250 | THE STORY OF VIC & SADE

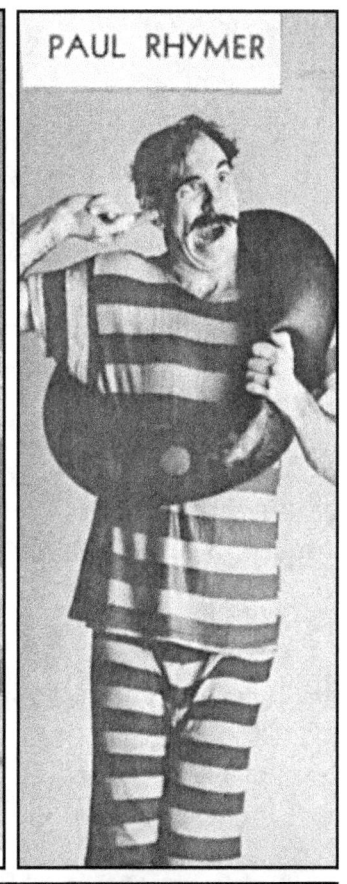

SUGGESTED FRONTISPIECE for your 2d. book

William Idelson, the author, and Paul Rhymer, the protagonist, are shown in native Breton costume performing the autochthonous rigadoon, "Mother Baker's Fire Stomp."

Mr William Idelson
5448 White Oak
Encino
California

February 3, 1936

SADE: (*Clears Throat*) Dear sister an' all: thought I would write an' see how you are feeling. We are fine. Has it been as cold down there as it has up here? Our thermometer registered fourteen below zero Monday of last week. The pipes in Walter's barber shop froze an' bursted. It will cost him seven dollars to repair the damage. Our next door neighbor's little boy had a toe to get frost-bit, an' our milk-man may lose the use of his hair. I haven't minded . . .

VIC: How's that? The milk-man what?

SADE: Lost the use of his hair.

VIC: Of his hair?

SADE: Yeah. "I haven't minded the cold so much, but Walter . . ."

VIC: How could he lose the use of his hair?

SADE: Got it frozen, I s'pose.

VIC: Ya mean it froze solid an' then chipped off?

SADE: I don't know, Vic. Why don'tcha let me read this?

VIC: I'm disturbed about that milk-man. If he lost the use of his hair he . . .

SADE: Maybe it was "head."

VIC: He lost the use of his head?

SADE: (*Looking Closely*) Could be "head." Bess kinda made a blotch here.

VIC: I'd say the milk-man kinda made a blotch. If he's lost the use of his head he . . .

SADE: Oh, what do you care. You don't know him.

VIC: I'd like to though. A guy that's had his head froze off would be worth money to the Ringling Brothers circus. Put him in a cage an' charge . . .

SADE: You wanta hear the rest of this?

VIC: I'll say.

Frank Walsh and I went to Arlington a few Saturdays ago and I won for a fucking change. I won only forty-odd bucks but it was refreshing. The races are a rotten delusion but a thought like this can't help occurring to your typical half-wit: if a guy bet $40 on three races in a row, each one paying off at 10 to 1, he'd have $40,000. No, I don't mean that. I mean he starts with forty and parlays his winnings each time. That would give him $40,000. And three 10-1 shots in a row isn't an unusual thing. The thing is that I'd never in the world have the guts.

I've stopped twice at Hartzel's house recently coming home from the farm but he wasn't there. Speaking of the farm I'm selling a fractional acre of it to a neighbor for a home-site. It's a slice of creek pasture we've never used and I'm getting $1,000. Let's see, at Arlington on a 10-1 shot I'd have $10,000. Parlaying that on the next race I'd have $100,000. On the third 10-1 race I'd have . . . Where's my hat? I'll finish this later.

The Carlson kids are over visiting at Donahue's and Mr. Donahue just got in off his St. Louis freight run an hour ago, so he asked once again if he could flake out on Sade's davenport. He's in there asleep when Vic and Rush come home. Vic grumbles that

Donahue always seems to be cluttering up their davenport, but Sade replies that it's only human decency to help a poor neighbor who needs sleep. Vic and Rush need to get into the living room, Rush for a copy of Scott's "Lady of the Lake," Vic for the newspaper, and Sade tells them to be very quiet. They enter the living room, regard Donahue, let their minds take wing a little with ideas of what could be done with the sleeping man, give voice to some insults to Donahue, voiced low enough not to wake him. Rush philosophizes a little about the oddities of sleep, and then:

RUSH: But he was a baby once. Might have been a pretty baby even. An' now look at him. Size eleven shoes—whiskers—cigars stickin' out of his pocket—hair in his ears—great big hands with . . .

VIC: I beg your pardon, Pete.

RUSH: Yeah?

VIC: What's that thing on the clip attached to your sweater there?

RUSH: Pencil.

VIC: Really? Soft lead?

RUSH: Very soft.

VIC: (*Pleasantly*) Well.

RUSH: Why?

VIC: Just wondered.

RUSH: You . . . got an idea up your sleeve?

VIC: Oh, no. Seein' that pencil though brought to mind

	a story I once heard about some mean nasty boys that drew a mustache on a man.
RUSH:	Drew a mustache on a man that was asleep?
VIC:	Yes . . . The young crooks.
RUSH:	Ah . . . Uh-huh.
VIC:	I hope you're not that kind of a boy.
RUSH:	Should say not.
VIC:	'Course it wasn't anybody's business but theirs. If they chose to take the highway to crime an' evil-doin' well, that's up to them.
RUSH:	Naturally.
VIC:	I'm a great stickler for mindin' my own affairs. Why, if somebody come in here this very minute with a pencil an' drew a mustache on uncle Donahue here, I'd never in the wide world move one muscle to interfere.
RUSH:	No?
VIC:	I should say not.
RUSH:	Well . . . a . . . Whatcha lookin' at?
VIC:	That picture over there on the wall. Never paid much attention to it before.
RUSH:	How long ya plan on lookin' at it?
VIC:	Oh, minute or two.

RUSH: Uh-huh.

VIC: Them cruel thoughtless boys I mentioned used a light quick stroke. It makes a much better lookin' mustache.

RUSH: O.K.

VIC: They were especially careful not to blow their breath in the face of the sleeping individual. Might wake him up.

RUSH: Yeah.

VIC: Yes sir, that's a might nice picture there on the wall. We oughta have more pictures like that.

RUSH: Yes, we should.

VIC: Next time I'm down town I think I'll drop in Yamilton's picture department an' see if they haven't got some more . . .

RUSH: Gov.

VIC: Yes, my boy?

RUSH: Somebody has been in here drawin' a mustache on Mr. Donahue.

VIC: The fiends. Let's see.

RUSH: (*Chuckling*) Not a bad mustache either.

VIC: (*Chuckling*) A good mustache. A fine mustache. (*Serious*) But if I ever find the rotten crooks that perpetrated this outrage I'll . . .

SADE: (*Coming In*) Dinner, boys.

RUSH: (*To Vic*) Oh, gosh.

VIC: (*To Rush In Low Tones*) You accuse me an' I'll accuse you.

RUSH: That the best way?

VIC: Yes. (*Raises Voice*) We're coming, kiddo, we . . .

SADE: (*Coming Up*) What's going on here?

VIC: Nothing at all. George an' I were just discussing a little matter that . . .

SADE: (*Almost Up*) How would you like to go to somebody's house to rest a while an' have people standin' over ya like . . . (*Sees The Mustache*)

VIC: (*After A Brief Pause*) Did you say dinner was ready, kiddo?

SADE: (*Silent*)

VIC: Rush, your mother has announced dinner. Shall we repair to the . . .

SADE: Who done this?

VIC: Done what?

SADE: I say who done this?

VIC: You mean . . .

SADE: You know what I mean. Who done it?

VIC:	Rush.
SADE:	Rush, I'm gonna give you just . . .
RUSH:	Gov did it.
SADE:	Gov drew this mustache?
RUSH:	Yes.
SADE:	Vic, for a great big man that's s'posed to have . . .
VIC:	Rush did that.
RUSH:	Gov did it.
VIC:	Don't hide behind papa's skirts, George. Own up.
RUSH:	You own up.
VIC:	C'mon—tell your mother the truth.
RUSH:	You tell her the truth.
SADE:	Vic, who done this?
VIC:	Rush.
RUSH:	Gov.
VIC:	Rush.
RUSH:	Gov.
SADE:	All right, fellas.
VIC & RUSH:	Huh?

SADE:	C'mon an' eat your dinner. I see my troubles are just beginning. I thought I had two men. I find out I got two five-year olds. C'mon.
ANOTHER JOKE:	A bride of two months walked into the bathroom and saw her husband taking an ice-cold shower. She stared at his wizened foreshortened cock in horror. "My God, is that all we got left out of what we started with on our wedding night?"

Rush interrupted once too often this evening and was sent to his room. But a short time later he emerges to say that it's absolutely imperative he be allowed to make a telephone call . . .

GRAN'PA SNYDER HAS FRIEND OVER   FEBRUARY 18, 1936

SADE:	Tell what you got to tell, Rush, an' then go back to your room.
RUSH:	It's Gran'pa Snyder I wanta telephone.
SADE:	(*Briefly*) You said that.
RUSH:	I . . . He's got a friend visitin' him tonight. This friend is almost eighty-five years old just like Gran'pa. They were boys together a long long time ago. An' they never get to see each other but about once every ten years or so. This friend lives with his married son in Colfax Illinois an' they kinda keep a tight rein on him . . . never let him leave the house much. About the way Gran'pa Snyder's daughters keep their finger on Gran'pa, ya know?
SADE:	Well?
RUSH:	It just happens that this old man has been feelin' pretty good recently and his son let him ride from

	Colfax in a milk-truck. To see Gran'pa Snyder. Well, Gran'pa Snyder knew he was comin' so he got his daughters to sorta let up the pressure a little.

SADE: How ya mean?

RUSH: You know how they handle him. They love him an' all, but they do kinda treat him like a baby.

SADE: He's awful awful old.

RUSH: He don't feel so awful old. In fact, the other day he wanted to plot out a horse-shoe court an' . . .

SADE: (*Impatiently*) Well, what's all this about? You're supposed to be upstairs in your room.

RUSH: I'll . . . hurry the story along.

SADE: Yeah.

RUSH: Like I said, Gran'pa's daughters treat him like a baby. They always got him bundled up in robes, an' they pick out the stuff they want him to eat, an' they're careful not to say anything to excite him, an' they humor him an' . . . Well, you know.

SADE: (*Assent*) Um.

RUSH: But here's this old friend comin' tonight. Well, Gran'pa don't want his friend to see him bein' carted around like he was helpless. Old guys like that are kinda jealous of each other about who's the youngest an' peppiest. Gran'pa wants his friend to think he's full of ginger an' carryin' on big business affairs an' havin' a swell time an' not having' a free minute to do anything an' . . . Well, you know.

SADE: (*Assent*) Um.

RUSH: So Gran'pa got his daughters to let him sit in the parlor tonight to entertain his friend. Generally he don't get to sit in the parlor because he's careless with his chewin' tobacco, an' when company's around he wants to do all the talkin' . . . an' like that.

SADE: Uh-huh.

RUSH: But tonight he's gonna have the run of the house. His daughters are gonna let him sit in the parlor an' play the radio an' serve refreshments. An' Gran'pa's got a ten-dollar bill wrapped around some newspaper to look like a wad of bills he's gonna flourish. An' ya know Grace?

SADE: The hired girl?

RUSH: Yeah. She's agreed to take orders from Gran'pa tonight.

SADE: Um. Where do you come in on all this?

RUSH: I promised Gran'pa I'd telephone.

SADE: Telephone what?

RUSH: Any ol' thing. Just so the phone rings an' it's somebody wantin' to speak to Gran'pa.

SADE: Oh.

RUSH: Do you catch on to what I'm tryin' to get across?

SADE: Gran'pa wants it to look like people are tryin' to get in touch with him all the time?

RUSH: That's the idea exactly. See, this other ol' guy'll be impressed. He'll go back to Colfax thinkin' Gran'pa Snyder is red-hot potatoes.

SADE: (*Giggles*)

RUSH: (***Gets Courage From Her Giggle And Laughs***)

SADE: How many times ya gonna call him?

RUSH: I promised him half a dozen.

SADE: Oh, my.

RUSH: See, he'll let on to his friend that it's the Mayor an' the fire-chief an' the guy from the bank an' a lady that's kinda sweet on him an' a whole gang of big-shots.

SADE: (***Who's Forgotten Her Peeve***) Poor ol' fella.

RUSH: Poor ol' fella is right. Here he is puttin' on this great big show for his friend.

SADE: His friend might have a trick or two up his sleeve also.

RUSH: I wouldn't doubt it. I wouldn't doubt it.

SADE: (***Enjoys A Friendly Laugh With Her Son***) And when they're through . . . Vic, have you heard all this about . . . (***Sees His Eyes Are Closed***) Vic. (***Pause***) Vic.

RUSH: Guess he's asleep.

SADE: Yeah, he is.

RUSH: (***Back To Gran'pa***) He ain't in such a bad spot though, Mom.

SADE: Who, Gran'pa Snyder?

RUSH: Yeah. I hope I got nice daughters like his to look after me when I'm his age.

SADE: Who's gonna look after Gov an' me? We got no daughters.

RUSH: (*Reassuringly*) Don't worry about that, sister.

SADE: (*Enjoys A Laugh With Her Son*)

RUSH: Well—guess I better get at my phone callin'. It's past eight o'clock.

SADE: Want me to help you?

RUSH: Help me?

SADE: I can be the lady that's kinda sweet on Gran'pa.

RUSH: Swell. (*Laughs*)

SADE: (*Laughs*)

RUSH: I'll call him first, huh?

SADE: All right.

RUSH: Ah . . . Mom.

SADE: Yeah?

RUSH: I . . . This evening when I . . . About after supper tonight . . . I mean . . . Well, shucks.

SADE: Go on: what'd ya start to say?

RUSH: Nothin', I guess. We don't need to say anything to each other, Mom. We kinda got each other doped out an' understand.

End of Script

ANNOUNCER: Which concludes another brief interlude at the small house half-way up in the next block. (*Pause*)

Closing and Commercial Credits

Jack Dunn

June 29, 1959

I play chess one evening a week with Jack Dunn. I don't know whether you remember Jack Dunn or not. Jack recently went through bankruptcy. He owed some thousands of dollars and now he doesn't owe anybody anything. His creditors included four doctors and a loan company. There was a meeting at the court house to share Jack's assets on a pro rata basis but since Jack owed me only $25 and the loan company $600 (besides 35 other folks to whom he owed varying amounts) and since Jack's assets were a beat-up card table thought to be worth $1.75 in the market I decided it wouldn't be worth my while to attend that meeting. Jack's eyes are like hot agates as he gazes down at his cool green salad. Frequently he extends his slender foot in its smart shoe.

Rooster Davis is an acknowledged genius at getting out of work at school. His skill at thinking up dodges that completely sidetrack the routine of education is nothing less than fantastic. It was Rooster, for instance, who conceived the plan of having the graduating class spend most of a day writing about what they'd do for Edwards School when they became rich and famous. And Mis' Kinney bought it!

Now in high school, Rooster has lost none of his skill. Today they were asked to write an essay, but naturally his first thought went to the avoidance of same:

Rooster's Genius   March 17, 1936

VIC: Rooster figured out he was the ninth guy to get called on an' there was only time for eight themes to be read. So he never prepared any theme?

RUSH: Yeah. That was the first example of genius.

VIC: An' then there was a hitch in his plot when two girls turned up absent.

RUSH: Right. He got called on anyway.

VIC: Proceed.

RUSH: So here's the picture:—It's two minutes until time for the bell to ring. Mis' Shade says, "Now we'll hear Edwin Davis' report on Illinois glacial formations." Edwin Davis rises to his feet. He ain't got any more report on Illinois glacial formations than a rabbit. He's got to think fast. He opens up his geography book takin' plenty of time to find a certain page. He does the same thing with his algebra. Does the same thing with his Latin. He reaches in his pocket an' pulls out a letter. He spread his letter on his desk. He whips out his pencil. He makes several notes. He's organizin' his material, get the angle?

VIC: Sure.

RUSH: So he picks up his copy of "The Last of the Mohicans," covering it up as much as he can with his hand so the title don't show. He's lettin' on it's a library book. He opens his mouth like he's gonna read an' discovers he's got the wrong page. He finds the right page. He digs down in his pocket for another wad of paper. He pulls out the Y.M.C.A. basketball schedule. He refers to it. He glances

	back at his algebra book. He opens his mouth an' says, "A Report on the Glacial Formations of Illinois." An', Gov.
Vic:	Uh-huh.
Rush:	Guess what happened next.
Vic:	What happened next?
Rush:	The bell rang.
Vic:	Rooster was saved. Genius.
Rush:	Ain't that genius though?
Vic:	And how.
Rush:	Sheer genius.
Vic:	Sheer genius. Well—let's find the meat loaf.

End of Script

Announcer:	Which concludes another brief interlude at the small house half-way up in the next block. (*Pause*)

Closing and Commercial Credits

And McClaughery delivered himself of this at a recent business man's lunch: "Yeah, Gloria Swanson. I wonder how Gloria Swanson would like to have 15/16 of an inch of hard cock stuck up her twat. Not one sixteenth. Not two sixteenth. Not three sixteenths. Not four sixteenths. Just keep counting, buster!"

Paul never visited a psychiatrist. "I can't see telling all my innermost secrets to some guy I hardly know," he said. But he was psychiatrically oriented, all right, if that meant being intensely aware of the real feelings and motivations behind the things we do and say.

After A 500 Game   April 7, 1936   Tuesday

INTRODUCTION: Well sir, we have no scene as we enter the small house half-way up in the next block now, because within the largest upstairs bedroom where we are taking you it is pitch dark and almost twelve o'clock midnight. But here's a voice. Listen.

SADE: (*Softly*) Vic?

VIC: (*With A Bare Edge Of Gruffness*) What?

SADE: Asleep?

VIC: Yeah.

SADE: No, you're not.

VIC: Yes, I am.

SADE: Talk to me a minute.

VIC: I'm very drowsy.

SADE: Vic, I don't wanta go to sleep mad.

VIC: Whatcha mad about?

SADE: I'm not mad. But you are.

VIC: Me? Mad? Laughable. My soul never was so much at peace. I never was so serene.

SADE: Fred don't mean to be aggravating.

VIC: Sade, you'll kindly not mention that name to me again. I've finished with Fred Stembottom. I play no more Five Hundred with Fred Stembottom. I brush no more elbows with Fred Stembottom. Fred Stembottom an' I are quits.

SADE: I know you feel bad about tonight.

VIC: (*With Spirit*) Who feels bad about tonight? I don't feel bad about tonight. I feel good about tonight. Tonight has taught me that a man can cherish a rattle-snake as a friend an' . . .

SADE: A little lower, Vic.

VIC: Huh?

SADE: You'll wake Rush up talkin' so loud.

VIC: Very well, I'll say no more. Let us sleep. I bid you good-night. (*With Finality*) Good night.

SADE: (*After A Brief Pause*) It's just his way.

VIC: What's just who's say?

SADE: It's just Fred's way to get under a person's skin.

VIC: He didn't get under my skin. He might of thought he got under my skin, but he didn't get under my skin.

SADE: Jokin' is all it really is. I realize that kind of jokin' bothers a person.

VIC: It didn't bother me by a long shot.

SADE: (*Timidly*) You got kinda red in the face.

VIC:	(*Tough*) What?
SADE:	You . . . kinda squirmed in your chair when he was talkin'.
VIC:	(***Louder Than Necessary***) Who wouldn't squirm around in their chair listenin' to such ignorant bunk? Who wouldn't . . .
SADE:	Please, Vic—Rush.
VIC:	(***Referring To Fred***) The fat-head.
SADE:	(***Brief Pause***) It's just Fred's way.
VIC:	Just his way, hey? Some way. I'll say. (***A Poem***)
SADE:	I know he's stubborn an' loud-talkin' but he's a wonderful husband to Ruthie an' such a good provider an' sends money to his folks an' just as soon give you the shirt off his back as . . .
VIC:	I don't want the shirt off his back. I wouldn't have the shirt off his back. An' I'll tell ya this, Sade. I've been in that guy's house for the last time. The—last—time.
SADE:	I bet if he had any idea you felt this way about it, he'd just more'n apologize. I bet he'd come over a-kittin' sayin' how sorry he . . .
VIC:	If he come over a-kittin' I'd send him right back again a-kittin'. Listen, were we or were we not guests at his home tonight?
SADE:	'Course we were guests in his home tonight an' that's why I say . . .

VIC: Let me say a minute . . . long as we're gonna lay in bed till morning talking. We were guests over there tonight. We were invited over there to play a sociable game of cards. What did our courteous host do? He lit right in an' told his guest his business was just so much hooey. He spent twenty minutes laughin' about his guest's . . .

SADE: No, he didn't Vic. He . . .

VIC: (*Exercised*) He didn't? He didn't? Fred Stembottom didn't sit there at that card-table with that big wide dumb half-wit grin on his face an' snort over how funny my job down at the Plant . . .

SADE: Vic, please. You're talkin' terrible loud. Rush's got to have his sleep.

VIC: O.K. I didn't ask to discuss this. You're the one that wanted to have a pleasant chat in the middle of the night.

SADE: Couldn't you bring your voice down just a little?

VIC: I'll bring my voice down to nothin'. I need sleep myself. I bid you good-night. Good-night.

SADE: (*Ignoring This*) Fred didn't laugh at your job, Vic.

VIC: Oh, he didn't, huh? Where were you? In Canada? He sat there with that monkey-face grin an' went on for twenty minutes about the Kitchenware Industry. (*Mocks Fred*) "How do they get men to go in Kitchenware, Vic? Do they pick 'em out of insane asylums or do they stunt the brains of new-born babies?"

SADE: He just meant that to be funny.

VIC:		Did you think it was funny?
SADE:		No, but . . .
VIC:		I should think it'd burn you up to hear cheap cracks like that about your husband's work.
SADE:		I didn't think it was very smart of Fred to go on like that, but just the same I realized he was only . . .
VIC:		We make our living out of Kitchenware. The food we eat comes from Kitchenware. Our money in the bank comes from Kitchenware. I've spent going on twenty years of my life in Kitchenware. All the future I got is Kitchenware.
SADE:		No, I didn't think it was very smart of Fred to go on like that but just the same I realized . . .
VIC:		An' who the heck is Fred Stembottom? Nothin' but a rotten little thirty-two-dollar-a-week clerk that only hangs on to his job because his bosses are too kind-hearted to . . .
SADE:		(*Reproach*) Oh, Vic.
VIC:		Oh, I wouldn't tell that to him. I wouldn't tell it to nobody. But what if I had said things like that tonight? He did. To me.
SADE:		(*Small Voice*) Only foolin' though.
VIC:		(*Scornfully*) "Only foolin'." "Only foolin'."
SADE:		Well, he was only foolin'. I know Fred's a little stupid when it comes to lots of things but I know as sure as there's a man in the moon that he wouldn't set out to hurt . . .

VIC: What surprises me, Sade, is that you didn't get mad yourself. That's what surprises me.

SADE: I did get a little mad. I . . .

VIC: Certainly acted it. You an' Ruthie both sat there an' giggled while Fred was hittin' up the two-bit comedy. Laughed out loud when he called me "The Prince of Pots an' Pans" an' the "Sweetheart of the Fryin' Skittle."

SADE: I laughed because . . .

VIC: Never mind. It's O.K. It won't happen again. I've been in Fred Stembottom's house for the last time an' you can put that in your pipe an' smoke it. Now let's go to sleep. Must be going on one o'clock.

SADE: Vic, don't get mad, but . . .

VIC: I'm not mad.

SADE: Don't you . . . Can't you kinda see where . . . Don't get mad now at what I say, will ya?

VIC: I'm not mad. I'm not mad. Can't I kinda see what?

SADE: Can't you kinda see where maybe you were a little bit half to blame tonight?

VIC: How?

SADE: Fred didn't start his joshin' till . . . till after you give him a little joshin'.

VIC: Did I run down his job? Did I make fun of the way he makes a living? Did I poke him in the spot where it hurts the worst?

SADE: No, but . . . (*Halts*)

VIC: But what?

SADE: You kinda went after his goat early in the evening there.

VIC: When?

SADE: Well—remember when Ruthie served the ice cream?

VIC: I do.

SADE: Remember what was bein' said?

VIC: I complimented Ruthie on her ice cream, stated it was delicious, announced it was my favorite flavor, an' in every way behaved like a guest is s'posed to behave.

SADE: Do you remember—I may not get this exactly right—but do you remember sayin' you liked ice cream served in round chunks like baseballs?

VIC: I do.

SADE: An' then you recollect what Fred said?

VIC: Somethin' insulting, I imagine. What'd he say?

SADE: He said speakin' of baseball it wouldn't be long now before . . . Crazy Bean, is it?

VIC: Dizzy Dean.

SADE: He said speakin' of baseball it wouldn't be long now before Dizzy Dean would be fannin' out National League batters like sick flies.

VIC: I recall the remark, yes.

SADE: An' then you said Dizzy Dean was just so much wet gun powder an' oughta be plowin' corn down on the farm.

VIC: Sure. That's right. Dizzy Dean's a flash in the pan.

SADE: That got under Fred's skin.

VIC: What did?

SADE: The things you said about Dizzy Dean. He thinks Dizzy Dean is marvelous. Keeps a scrap book about him an' everything. Listens to the radio. Thinks the sun rises an' sets on Dizzy Dean.

VIC: That's another example of Fred's stupidity.

SADE: But you were trompin' on his toes with the things you said.

VIC: Good.

SADE: Trampin' on 'em good an' hard. I saw his neck get red as fire one time there when you said you'd rather have one pitcher from the bush league than all the Dizzy Deans in the world.

VIC: I was tellin' the truth. I would.

SADE: But it made Fred mad.

VIC: Excellent.

SADE: An' you went right ahead makin' him mad. You were talkin' about his car. Said you'd bet him three to one the transmission wouldn't hold up five hundred miles.

Vic:	An' it won't. I was statin' facts. Everybody knows that make of automobile is so much junk.
Sade:	But after all it's his car. He paid good money for it. He's as proud of it as Adam. Goes over it with a damp cloth every night of the universe.
Vic:	If he was smarter he'd drive it in Sugar Crick.
Sade:	But don't you see, Vic?
Vic:	See what?
Sade:	He didn't make you any madder than you made him. It was just one thing leading to another. Till finally he got on the subject of Kitchenware.
Vic:	Well, he won't get on the subject of Kitchenware any more. Not with me. I'm through with the fat-head.
Sade:	But won't you admit you were partly to blame for . . .
Vic:	Kiddo, it's getting' on for morning. Let's get some sleep.
Sade:	All right.
Vic:	Good night.
Sade:	Good night.

(*Pause*)

(*More Pause*)

Sade:	Vic.

VIC: I'm asleep.

SADE: It's Ruthie that I'm thinking of.

VIC: What about her?

SADE: She's my best friend.

VIC: Well?

SADE: I wouldn't lose her for anything.

VIC: You don't hafta lose her.

SADE: (*Pause*) When you an' Fred have these flare-ups, naturally the wife sticks to the husband. I noticed it tonight. I was peeved when Fred was laughin' at your work an' Ruthie was peeved when you were makin' fun of Fred's baseball players an' his auto. We just couldn't help it. We tried to, but it was bound to show a little. Like I said, Ruthie is my best friend. My very best friend. I'm with other ladies a lot, yes—Mis' Donahue an' Mis' Harris an' Mis' Brighton an' Mis' Appelrot—but it's not the same. Maybe it's because they're a little older than I am. Maybe it's because they're a little brighter in the head an' got more education. I don't know what it is. But I'm not the same with them as I am with Ruthie. With Ruthie I can laugh an' cry an' fight an' gossip an' talk nonsense an' just get along marvelous. With other ladies I sorta feel like here I am a woman that ain't a girl any longer an' got a fourteen year old boy to boot. See?

VIC: Um.

SADE: Ruthie an' I get along a lot like kids get along. It's hard for married ladies with families to have close

	friends where you can just take your hair down. An' Ruthie's the only close friend like that I got. The only one I ever will have probably . . . because I'm getting along to an age where women don't make close friends. (*Pause*) Awake?
VIC:	Yeah—I'm listenin'.
SADE:	You . . . see what I mean?
VIC:	Uh-huh.
SADE:	Don't you think . . . If you tried don't you think you an' Fred could hit it off better?
VIC:	I guess so.
SADE:	Mean it?
VIC:	Sure. Fred ain't beyond redemption. Not a bad egg at all if ya don't take him serious.
SADE:	Would it . . . Would it be all right if . . . (***Low Giggle Because She's Afraid To Say It***)
VIC:	Would it be all right if what?
SADE:	If I asked 'em over tomorrow night for more cards?
VIC:	Fred an' Ruthie?
SADE:	Yes.
VIC:	Sure.
SADE:	You're not just talkin'?

VIC:	No. Go ahead—ask 'em over.
SADE:	Thanks, Vic.
VIC:	Hey, kiddo, don'tcha think we oughta settle down an' get some sleep?
SADE:	Yes.
VIC:	Good-night.
SADE:	Good-night.

END OF SCRIPT

ANNOUNCER:	Which concludes another brief interval at the small house half-way up in the next block. (*Pause*)

CLOSING AND COMMERCIAL CREDITS

MAY 15, 1944

> I am very fat. I haven't smoked for over a year. I play lots of chess with my neighbor Ed Block downstairs. I play with myself lots. I don't know whether Ed Block my neighbor downstairs plays with himself lots or not. I miss you, Harry, and wish we could take a ride together on Saturday.

Mildred Tinsdel has noticed changes in Rush's face:

RUSH'S FEATURES CHANGING TO MAN'S   August 19, 1936

VIC:	What changes has she noticed?
RUSH:	Well, a while back I had a child's face. Soft an' sweet, ya know?

SADE: (*Mixed Amusement An' Disgust*) Oh, Rush, for heavens sake.

RUSH: That's a fact. I don't say I had a pretty face. I just say I had a child's face. Melting—unformed—tender—lovable.

VIC: How'd you like to put your lovable unformed face in your hat an' pull your hat down over your ears?

RUSH: (*Good-Naturedly*) That's O.K., Gov. Can't get my goat. But what I'm sayin' is the truth. Mildred noticed the change an' I've just checked up on her by observing my reflection in this lookin' glass. No longer have I the face of a child.

SADE: What kind of a face ya got?

RUSH: My features have arranged themselves in the hard granite lines of manhood.

SADE: Let's see some of them lines.

RUSH: Notice here how the firm flesh hugs the neck?

SADE: (*Giggling*) Sure. That firm flesh is huggin' away to beat the band.

RUSH: Notice how my chin has taken on a stronger richer curve.

SADE: There's a dirty curve there I see. You wash that lovable unformed face before you sit down to the table.

RUSH: I will. The thing Mildred noticed particularly was my eyes.

SADE:	What'd she notice.
RUSH:	The warm appealing brown-ness of helpless childhood has given way to the flashing hot fire of do-or-die courage an' the blue-steel glint of ambitious thunder an' . . .
SADE:	Hey, I believe I've heard enough of this.
VIC:	Believe I have myself.
RUSH:	(*Good Naturedly*) O.K. O.K. Just tellin' ya was all.
VIC:	S'pose that meat's done, kiddo?
SADE:	Let's go see. C'mon, Rush, bring that sweet lovable face of yours in the house an' wash it.

END OF SCRIPT

ANNOUNCER:	Which concludes another brief interlude at the small house half-way up in the next block. (*Pause*)

CLOSING AND COMMERCIAL CREDITS

I like whiskey fine. It rises rapidly to the higher nervous centers and induces a sense of satisfaction.

Donahue, it seems, has now taken some things for granted, and it's made Sade mad. There was company at his house and he needed sleep, just having got in off some freight drag or other, and, though Sade was not home to ask, he came in an plopped himself down on her davenport and went to sleep. Sade herself has company coming and would like Vic to wake Donahue up and tell him he can't sleep on the davenport this afternoon. It's a task Vic accepts with a rather strange eagerness . . .

Donahue Asleep—He Didn't Ask   November 19, 1936

SADE: (*Opening Door*) An' don't let on to Mr. Donahue how I feel.

VIC: No sir.

SADE: Just tell him nice an' polite Mrs. Gook is expecting company.

VIC: Right.

SADE: An' I'll be back in just a few minutes.

VIC: Right.

(*Door Slam*)

RUSH: (*To Vic*) I'm in on this, ya know?

VIC: In on what?

RUSH: In on wakin' Mr. Donahue up.

VIC: O.K. I can use a bright assistant. Shall we repair to the living room an' look over the ground?

RUSH: O.K.

VIC: Lead the way.

RUSH: How about the matches an' thumb-tacks an' cold water? I've got a little idea where ya take milk bottle tops an' smear 'em with butter an' . . .

VIC: Let's inspect our victim first. Then we can gather together props an' paraphernalia.

RUSH: Don't forget Mom'll be back in five minutes.

VIC: Julius Caesar defeated the Carthaginians an' destroyed an empire in five minutes.

RUSH: Well, you're the boss, I guess.

VIC: I'm the boss an' I'm gonna see that this job is polished off right.

RUSH: I got a few schemes myself.

VIC: We must keep one golden ideal before us: we mustkeep in mind as we go about our work that Neighbor Donahue must never again feel inclined to break into peoples' private homes an' stretch out on people's private davenports.

RUSH: I think we can do it.

VIC: Ah—by the way, Axle-grease, haven't we got some fly-paper in the house?

RUSH: Sure.

VIC: Know where it is?

RUSH: Yeah—upstairs.

VIC: Go get it for Father.

RUSH: (*Chuckles*) O.K.

VIC: An' also bring down the dry-cell batteries on the attic steps, the small bottle of iodine in the bath-room, a pair of suspenders, your mother's hair-curler, three hair pins, an' a shoe-horn.

End of Script

ANNOUNCER: Which concludes another brief interlude at the small house half-way up in the next block. (*Pause*)

Closing and Commercial Credits

Feb. 11, 1958

Vic and Sade continues to reverberate. On two of the Jack Paar shows they devoted considerable time to eulogy and I'm told Bill Cullen plays **Vic and Sade** records on a New York early morning radio show.

Peggy asked me over recently to go through a bureau drawer of Art's containing material having to do with the program. She also offered me Art's gold pocket watch as a keepsake. I accepted it gratefully.

On December 8, 1936, Vic comes home with the news that Hank Gutstop has had a star named after him by Lodge Headquarters. Sade and Rush have a number of questions, of course, and in explanation Vic reads them the letter he received this morning . . .

VIC: Ah . . . (***Reads***) . . . "Dear sky-brother Gook: this is to advise you that Henry Gutstop of your chapter had the good fortune of having his name drawn at our ceremony last Friday. This means, of course, that sky-brother Gutstop is to have a star named after him. Will you kindly notify sky-brother Gutstop? The star has already been selected and can be located by determining a point seventy-three degrees an' forty minutes from the handle of the Big Dipper. A simpler method of finding the star is to follow with the eye an imaginary line directly to the left of the moon. The new Henry Gutstop star is the brightest one in that area. Please convey to sky-brother Gutstop our heartiest congratulations. Yours very truly.

SADE: Of all the wild notions them fellas can cook up.

VIC: I guess there's no point in our discussing the matter, Sade. Shall we go out in the alley now, Rush?

RUSH: All right.

VIC: Where's your overcoat?

RUSH: In the kitchen. I'll grab it on the way.

VIC: O.K. (*To Sade*) Kiddo, excuse us for a little while. We're going . . . You coming along?

SADE: Yeah. I like to have fun too.

VIC: This isn't an expedition for fun.

SADE: (*Giggles*) I want to see the star named Hank Gutstop.

VIC: I'm afraid I can't see my way clear to makin' you welcome if you plan to scoff.

SADE: You don't hafta bother makin' me welcome.

VIC: Neither do I intend to listen to wise-cracks.

SADE: Let's go if we're going.

RUSH: Cold outside, Mom. You'll need a coat.

SADE: I'll throw my heavy sweater over my shoulders.

VIC: I say I do not intend to listen to any wise-cracks, Sade.

SADE: All right.

RUSH: Was Hank pretty excited when you told him the good news, Gov?

VIC: Naturally. Wouldn't you be?

RUSH: I s'pose so.

VIC: Sure.

RUSH: Still an' all though, there ain't much profit in it.

VIC: There's other things in this world besides profit. Steam-heat. John Gutenberg didn't make much profits out of inventing the printing press but his name will last as long as civilization lasts.

RUSH: Will Hank Gutstop's name last that long?

VIC: I see no reason to doubt it.

RUSH: Just the same, though, if a guy was to come up to me an' say, "Gook, I'll name a star after ya or I'll give ya forty dollars, which do ya want?" I believe I'd take the forty dollars.

SADE: I bet Hank would too.

VIC: (*Coldly*) Are you sure you want to come along with us, Sade?

SADE: (*Breezily*) Uh-huh. Open the door, son.

RUSH: (*Opening It*) Ya think you pick out the right star, Gov?

VIC: The directions as given in the letter from headquarters seemed quite explicit.

RUSH: They said to follow with the eye an imaginary line to the left of the moon.

VIC: Right.

RUSH: There's a million stars to the left of the moon. (*Door Closes*)

SADE: Maybe they're all named Hank Gutstop.

VIC: (*Coldly*) I beg your pardon, Sade?

SADE: I say maybe all the stars to the left of the moon are named Hank Gutstop.

VIC: (*Coldly*) You'll forgive my not laughing?

SADE: Go right ahead an' don't laugh.

RUSH: Hey, there's stars by the gallon up in that sky. We'll never find Hank.

VIC: Let us proceed to the alley. I'll find Hank for ya.

SADE: Ruthie'll get lots of giggles out of this when I tell her.

VIC: You may tell Ruthie to put her giggles in her hat an' pull her hat down over her ears.

SADE: No, but she will, though. (*Giggles*) Imagine: that ol' hulk of a Gutsop that's always paddin' around town in tennis shoes havin' a star named after him.

VIC: Thomas A Edison padded around town in tennis shoes an' invented the telephone.

RUSH: It was Alexander Graham Bell invented the

	telephone, Gov. Thomas A. Edison invented the electric light an' the phonogra . . .
SADE:	Rush, there's Mr. Donahue.
RUSH:	Where?
SADE:	Dontcha see him up there in the sky? Just to the right of the moon?
RUSH:	You're bein' kidded, Gov. (*Chuckles*)
VIC:	Am I? Well, they kidded Napoleon also. But they didn't kid him much at the Battle of Waterloo.
RUSH:	They kidded him an awful lot at the Battle of Waterloo. Napoleon lost the Battle of Waterloo.
VIC:	I mean the Battle of Gettysburg or wherever the heck it was.
RUSH:	The Battle of Gettysburg was fought in the Civil War, Gov. You must be thinking of . . .
SADE:	Well, whatcha know!—There's Mr. Croucher's delivery boy.
RUSH:	(*Chuckles*) Where, Mom?
SADE:	Up in the sky. Didn't you know the Chief of Police had named a star after Mr. Croucher's delivery boy?
VIC:	Some people oughta go on the stage an' tell their funny jokes.
SADE:	(*Pertly*) Sure.

RUSH: Find Hank yet, Gov?

VIC: I'm not sure but what I have. See the moon?

RUSH: Yeah?

VIC: All right, look at the brightest star to the left of it.

RUSH: There's a bushel of stars in between.

VIC: Yeah, but no real bright ones. See the one I mean.

RUSH: Point to it.

VIC: Oh, "point to it"—how can a guy point to a star?

RUSH: Well, heck, I can't . . .

VIC: Do ya see the moon?

RUSH: Sure. (*Chuckles*) No trick to that.

SADE: Wonder what the lodge has named the moon.

RUSH: Herman D. Wilcox, I bet.

SADE: L.W. Hookerman.

RUSH: Heinie Johnson.

SADE: Why not just "Heinie"? (*They Laugh*)

VIC: When the laughter over these funny, funny, funny remarks has died down a little I'll show ya the star we're looking for.

SADE & RUSH: Where is it?

VIC: First locate the moon.

SADE & RUSH: (*Laughing*) That's not hard.

VIC: Do you wanta see Hank Gutstop or don't ya?

SADE: Where is he?

VIC: Imagine there's a straight line coming out of the moon to the left.

SADE: All right.

VIC: Done that?

SADE: Yeah.

VIC: O.K., the first bright star ya see in the path of that straight line is Hank.

RUSH: Oh, uh-huh.

VIC: See him?

RUSH: Yeah.

VIC: Do you, Sade?

SADE: Sure. I see Hank. Hello, Hank.

RUSH: (*Calls*) How ya feelin', Hank?

SADE: (*In A Small Voice As Though Far Away*) Fine.

RUSH: Must be hot stuff bein' way up there in the sky.

SADE: (*Small Voice*) Yeah, but the darn ol' moon bumps into me all the time.

RUSH: That's tough.

SADE: (*Small Voice*) Sure is. Say, can ya lend me fifteen cents til . . .

VIC: (*Coldly*) O.K., friends.

SADE: (*Natural Tones*) Whatcha say?

VIC: You've had your fun. How about going back in the house now?

SADE: You gonna stay out here by yourself?

VIC: Yes.

RUSH: I expect you're gonna commune with yourself under the great silent mysterious heavens. Ain't that the gag? Ain't you gonna look up at Hank Gutstop beamin' an' shinin' an' . . .

VIC: Beat it!

RUSH: C'mon, Mom. I think we better be on our way.

END OF SCRIPT

ANNOUNCER: Which concludes another brief interlude at the small house half-way in the next block. (*Pause*)

CLOSING AND COMMERCIAL CREDITS

Last Chapter

The show continued until September 1944, then was dropped by Proctor and Gamble and went off the air. The reason for its demise was that it lost its original character. In 1942 I went into the service and, as it would have been with the loss of any one of the three principals, the delicate balance was destroyed. Paul, loyal to the character of Rush, did not

replace him, but brought in a different character named Russell, who somehow never fitted into the picture. Then, to compensate, he gave voice to several incidental characters and proved that his instinct at the start to keep them silent had been right. The show became confusing, and un-listenable.

Yes, they took my show off the air. Proctor and Gamble said, 'To hell with your rotten program. Take that half-assed program and stick it up your ass.' Well hell, what do you expect of a radio program. This one lasted thirteen years damn near. And it wouldn't surprise me too much if it went back on. Ausitot, monsoor, ici sont les crayona de ma tante. Je me pense que Je voir piss en avant de Toledo Ohio.

It returned to the air, in its fifteen-minute form, in the summer of '45, as an evening show on CBS. Johnny Coons played the part of Rush until September when I was discharged from the Navy and took over the role again. But the show still contained a lot of speaking characters and was still hodgepodge. It ended as a fifteen minute radio show on December 7, 1945. In the summer of '46 it had another resurgence as a half-hour summer replacement for **Fibber McGee and Molly**, sponsored by Johnson's Wax. In its half-hour version, played for laughs before an audience, it was a curious mutation but not too felicitous a one. It went off the air in September of '46 and was never done again on radio.

There were several attempts to bring **Vic and Sade** to television. They failed for several reasons. For one thing, the show was never really adapted for television. Paul, for all his talent, had never worked in a visual medium and didn't understand what needed to be done. He imagined that the scripts could be done almost exactly in their radio form. For another thing, the scripts selected were all from later years, when the basic situation comedy ideas had all been exhausted and Paul had gone on to a more intellectualized comedy, more sedentary, wordier, directed strictly to the ear. So these attempts to physicalize what was thoroughly an auditory concept were rather weird. The last attempt, in 1956, probably made the most sense:

There's always some kind of Vic & Sade action in the wind and last week money was spent and enthusiasm was fired. The local NBC-TV boss conceived the notion of folks reading scripts like you'd sit and take turns reading Shakespeare. I thought the idea was ridiculous and said so. Others didn't and we went ahead. Well sir, we auditioned and it was fine. They had Art and Bern sitting in big winged chairs in front of a velvet drop. This was in magnificent color. They had fancy camera shots where you saw the reactions of the characters who weren't speaking. Exits and entrances were contrived. It was funny and came off and had a real showman-like atmosphere. NBC is making money talk with us. The thing might come to something: again it mightn't. Rush is played by a lad named Eddie Gilliland who is a lanky 18 with an uncertain voice but a real feel for what's going on, a sure sense of timing, and no precocious actorish traits. He doesn't bat in your league by a long shot but I believe he'll be adequate. The present thought is to go on locally and sustaining. The pay is peanuts but everybody looks to sponsorship and network. Art is currently in good health and this activity (with no memorizing and muscular exertion) is assessed as good for him. O.K., I've brought you up to date on that issue and it may never be mentioned again by anybody on the face of the earth.

To all intents and purposes Paul retired in 1945, although he didn't know it at the time. There were sporadic attempts to revive *Vic and Sade* and a few other short-lived projects—a stint of writing a five-minute nightly show for Cliff Norton, called "The Public Life of Cliff Norton," the longest sustained work he did after '45. There were offers to write other shows from time to time, and for several years he traveled to New York frequently to discuss formats and ideas with Madison Avenue people but it all came to dead ends. He once said to me with a shrug, "Maybe I've done my work. Keats did his by the time he was twenty-four."

His attitude was a mixture of relief, fatalistic acceptance and puzzlement. For so many years he and his show had sat on the top of the heap. Now radio had fled Chicago and the era that had spawned radio itself was changing. The time and place had left and Paul had stayed behind.

For all his wild imagination he was not a terribly adaptive creature professionally. He was solidly entrenched in the Chicago Radio Syndrome, where radio was King and no other part of show business was worth taking seriously. Sometimes when he was making a real attempt to keep an open mind, when someone was urging him to tackle television or films he'd say, "Well, I don't see why not. It's all show business." But it wasn't, and Paul became a dinosaur at forty.

But he continued to enjoy life thoroughly, and prospects for working again were not necessarily a great part of it. If people came to him with offers he might get interested or excited for a little while, but essentially he just enjoyed living and was glad that he could do it unencumbered by those awful deadlines. The small moments of life were for him now leisurely and good . . . the lunches with pals, driving to the farm, or somewhere else in the country. On a Saturday he'd call a friend (often Harry Monroe) and say, "Let's drive to Montpelier. I've got to go to Montpelier!" He enjoyed the out-of-the-way, ethnic restaurants: Phil Schmidt's, Matt Schuleins, where Matt himself came to your table and did card tricks, Al's Oriental Broilings, as well as the famous Red Star Inn and the Buttery in the Ambassador. He played a lot of chess and had more than a few drinks now and then. He wrote a lot of letters and cards. His correspondence was his outlet for written humor, and he did a lot of it. He read a great deal and sometimes corresponded with other authors. One of his favorites of this time was Ann Parrish, and he wrote several letters to her although she was quite ill and unable to correspond too well.

I'll salt my communiqué with little funnies.

GENTLEMAN: What do you think of sex?

LADY: I think it's a pain in the ass.

GENTLEMAN: Perhaps you're not doing it right.

Before I forget I must mention that we saw you on our TV machine in a *Dragnet* re-run. You were one of the bad guys. And you were excellent. "Here's Billy!" shouted whoever was watching and we came dashing out of the toilet and places. I scrutinized carefully the features of a man approaching the half-century mark but you didn't look one whole hell of a lot different. The ineradicable marks of the underwitted were still there, of course, but even time of course can't do anything about that. In my own case, although I am slightly over forty, the pretty girls scream bloody murder about how young and cute I am. And rich masses of high-piled hair continue to frame the delicate oval of my face.

It was a delight to hear your voice the other evening. Of course I detected the slight quaver that comes with age. I manage to hold up startlingly well. Don't let on to Joan Crawford or Deenah Droobin but there were only three five minute periods in November when I didn't have a hard-on.

One of his closest pals during these years was Frank Walsh, an agency man who worked at Campbell-Mithun and lived in Oak Park. Paul, Frank and I made a threesome many an afternoon at the race track, and Frank being nearer to Paul age-wise than I, more literate than I, and more articulate than I, was closer on many levels than I, a situation that caused me some jealousy when we were together. But in response to a plea from me, Frank wrote some personal notes about Paul, which seemed to me to be so accurate and perceptive, and depict aspects of Paul so much better than I've been able to (dat old jealousy again), I'd like to reproduce some of them here:

MARCH 28, 1971

Rhymer is a difficult personality to write about. So discreet, so all-protective was his sense of personal privacy that even intimates of 30 years, as I, could not claim to know him entire. He liked to keep, as you must know, his personal and professional lives on clearly separated bases. And he had a specially wicked (but always controlled) scorn for the talent agents, the MCA guys, the agency personalities who might presume to get the two mixed up. Indeed the cornerstone of our particular relationship was a mutual recognition of these zones of privacy. Although I worked in a related and parallel field in the ad agencies we rarely, if ever, traded technical or professional gab. Except for taking shots at the absurdities practiced by some of the leading personalities in radio and the commercial side of same. Once he got the idea, assurance, that you weren't going to ask him how much he made per year, what he paid for the new Packard or "Where do you get those funny ideas, Mr. Rhymer," he could be your friend for life.

Bill, what also makes it tough to write about old pal Paul is that you know he would have rated the above mild statement "a lot of crap." One of his many attractive facets was his quick and devastating rejection of anything like intellectual pretension. (Although I hope the above does not qualify as such.) He used to let the air out of my tires regularly when I attempted to put a philosophical gloss on anything that seemed to him to be just plain common sense or a matter-of-fact. And I could always bring him out fighting when I suggested, as I did regularly, if he crowded me too much, that he had a mind like a woman's, *i.e.*, one incapable of entertaining an abstract idea.

He had a clarity of vision, an objectivity, about people and things around him that I sometimes envied although I rarely permit myself that sentiment. A look at his enthusiasm in literature and reading in general underlines this quality of his mind.

You'll recall his life-long love affair with Dickens. While I wandered in the symbol-laden jungles of Joyce, Faulkner, Camus, he went surely to the realists. He insisted that the artist tell him directly what he had to say, tell him no riddles. His much-thumbed list of favorites would carry these names:

Ring Lardner ("'Shut up,' he explained."). James Gould Cozzens (with whom he corresponded briefly). John O'Hara (he counted *Appointment in Samarra* one of the greatest long before the critics nominated it as a classic). Edith Wharton, Ruth Suckow (he wore out a couple of copies of *The Folks* and turned me on to it). Anne Parrish (he could quote jewels from her endlessly much like your *Vic and Sade* fans can quote from years of shows). Charles Jackson (he admired *Lost Weekend* as one of the finest of modern novels and was much absorbed with Jackson's own personal battle with the booze). Tarkington, of course. (He could take you by the hand through scene after scene of *Seventeen* or *Alice Adams*. Having handled his lines yourself, so beautifully for years, you must agree that he could give that old master cards and spades and beat him at his own game in the evocation of revealed truth in the little house half-way up the next block.) And so on: Fitzgerald and Hemingway were not for him. He thought the former couldn't write and he derided the phony side of the self-conscious Poppa much before the critics built that angle into the stuff of Sunday Supplements.

We did agree at the summit on Tolstoy and Mann. He was a good literary playmate. We entered the arena with widely separated viewpoints and he could be quite caustic about, "Walsh drawing his sacerdotal (a word he loved) robes about him and engaging in near-beer Jesuitical vaporings."

We chose the race track as one of our playgrounds because of the unexpected privacy it afforded. I had a literary allusion swiped from John O'Hara that I used to trot out regularly in observation about the track: O'Hara said that the face of the gambler is "perpetually locked between fear and greed." And it is this massed transfixion, of course, that permits real privacy at the track. Alone amid 20,000 catatonic horseplayers you can do pretty much what you want. A splendid place for a continuing dialog—surpassed only by the cemeteries where Rhymer and I used to wander when the tracks were closed. But that's another part of the forest.

Paul loved the racy vocabulary. Once returning from Washington Park on the race track special we heard a disgruntled punter who had been missing on long shots all day, moan loudly: "Jesus! The chalk come in like trained pigs today." (Translation: the favorites won all the races.) "Chalk" as you must know is the player's shorthand for the favorite in the betting. It's a bit of detritus (and how Paul loved that one!) left over from the days of the hand bookies at the track who used up a lot of chalk recording on their slates the declining odds as the crowd bet the hot choice. Rhymer would love to set you right on the etymology of such specialized jargon. And he delighted in the horseplayer's compulsive use of the historical present tense. Phrases like, "He win laughin'" or "He win with his head in the boy's lap," became as beautiful and quotable to us as something out of Shelley. "The teamster give him a beautiful ride," was a benediction bestowed on the jockey if you had the winner but this was immediately converted into, "The teamster runs him all over the track," if you lose.

Old race track joke, a barside litany Rhymer loved to recite:

Paul, after cashing winning ticket:
>Have a drink Frank?
>Sure.
>Whisky or beer?
>Beer.
>Draft or bottle?
>Bottle.
>Or can?
>Bottle.
>Light or dark?
>Light.
>Schlitz or Bud?
>Schlitz.
>Glass or stein?
>Glass.
>Oh piss on it! Two Old Fitzgeralds, bartender.

You'll remember his most famous parlor trick: playing the piano with great expertise and élan but about 5 degrees off true. At our house it was a command performance, commanded by my wife and three daughters who were invariably fractured by this turn. In the mood, he'd almost always accept the invitation and with mock modesty. The repertoire was strictly fraternity house, late 20s: "Charmaine," "Sweetheart of Sigma Chi," "By the Waters of the Minnetonka," "At Sundown," and the boff closer, "Nola." This he played at dangerous speed with all the wrongest notes at the rightest times. He could paralyze any group with this act, undismayed by my dropped trays, rattling ice cubes and other fly-catching tricks. His shy acceptance of the applause was a masterpiece of smirked understatement.

His audience one night included a concert pianist of some small reputation who pronounced in awe, "My God, it takes talent to do that to a piano so nearly perfect, so surprisingly wrong."

Paul's own view of this trick is set forth in the following letter to my wife, charging us with lack of appreciation.

September 21, 1935

My Dear Betty:

Mary Frances and Parke arrived home on schedule Sunday afternoon. They patronized the Trans World Airlines and enjoyed comfortable accommodations aboard one of that company's powerful Constellations. Both travelers report that New York is a huge bustling city and that there are many attractions to beguile the out-of-towner. The antics of the lumbering grizzly bear in Central Park Zoo coaxed chuckles from tiny Parke, and Mary Fran was lavish in her praises of the Empire State Building which is ranked as one of the world's tallest structures. Several amusing incidents also helped to make the Manhattan visit rememberable and . . .

Betty, I think I'll speak right out. Why wasn't I asked to play the piano Thursday evening? I'm wondering what you are doing as you read this. Are you giggling maliciously—as I suspect—or can it be possible that the whole wretched farce was some sort of mental block on your part? Sifting all the factors I can think of I fear any credence I give the latter concept will have to be buttressed by strong explanations—extremely strong explanations.

On the dozens of occasions I have visited your Clinton Street home there has never been a single one during which I was not asked to render "The Waters of Minnetonka," "The Sweetheart of Sigma Chi," "Nola," and other favorites. It seemed to me overwhelmingly significant that on an evening when thirty or more stunning young ladies were being entertained not one word was uttered about the foolish little act I do—a little act I had come to believe was enormously relished by you and your family.

I whisper to myself that jealousy pure and simple is the basis for this most regrettable thing. Knowing that Frank could scarcely be expected to enchant the young women with his riddles, puns and topical chaff you quietly decided that no outsider should be permitted to monopolize the spotlight.

Imagine my situation! There I sat on the veranda—dressed especially for the party in my gay sports jacket—pantingly waiting for you to say, "Paul, I know the girls are eager to hear you play." But you didn't say it! And the minutes marched on, and the pretty eighteen-year-olds continued to arrive. I don't doubt you marked my agitation. At one point I lapsed—as I'm apt to do when excited—into rapid nervous French. After I left you that awful evening I parked my machine near the railroad tracks at Oak Avenue and sobbed my heart out.

All this is going to be hard to forgive, Betty. If you can make a case for yourself I'm certainly willing—nay eager—to hear it. In the meantime, regards to Frank, your youngest daughter Josephine*, and your frolicsome little dog, Margie.

Most Sincerely,

Paul Mills Rhymer

*The daughter's name is Johanna. The dog's was Mickey. Perfect example of the style he used on the piano and so nicely used in this letter.

Since I lived in California most of these years, and Paul in Chicago, our connection was almost entirely by letter. But Paul kept me up to date on the activities of our mutual friends.

My pal Jack Dunn with whom you lunched in Forest Park last year isn't enjoying such sunny health. He has a tumor pressing on his optic nerve. A man's optic nerve is inside his skull and an operation might be indicated. This involves cutting off the top of the head which might be dangerous. I am keeping my fingers crossed for old Jack. He is at Illinois Masonic Hospital undergoing intense tests. I hope those intensive tests show that

Jack needn't have his head cut off.

I'd always get a letter on the special occasions of his or my life. When Seemah and I got married he chose to write to her:

April 7, 1951

Darling Sister:

We may call you sister, mayn't we? William just sent us the big news.

I am gathering the family together and we should be in your arms by the 18th. The Terre Haute Idelsons are meeting us in Moline and we will travel on from there by automobile. I don't know how much room you have but the Idelson crowd doesn't stand on ceremony and we'll manage to jam up some way. Anyhow 'blood is thicker than water.'

Eugene (second from right in the photo) must have a bed to himself. He still has the trouble he acquired in the Navy and Doctor Rogers fears a lurking danger of infection. He will bring his own blankets, sheets, silverware and crockery.

We don't actually have to have it but if you and William can advance us $85.00 our trip to California will be a good deal easier.

Ethel (extreme left) is almost completely herself again. (No more screams and canvas restrainers and messes in the basement, tell Bill.) We don't feel she'll be any problem.

Now, for goodness sake, sis, don't go to any bother. All seven of us are common as old shoes; we'll get along with you newly-weds like a house-afire. By the way, Bill will be glad to learn that little Dorothy has outgrown that 'house a-fire' phase. We hide matches from her, of course, but she's older and smarter now and has only the epilepsy to fight.

We plan to stay with you folks until late August or early September. September 15th is the absolute deadline. There's a chance that there'll be eight of us. It depends on whether or not Edgar Idelson gets acquitted of that tiresome crime-against-nature charge in Toledo.

Until the 18th then, little sister.

Sweetest, sweetest love,

Ruth Anne Idelson

In 1949 Paul was diagnosed as a diabetic, a serious case. But so strong was his need for personal privacy, he told no one about his condition.
As Mary Fran says, "We were never permitted to share this news with friends . . . only late in life did Paul permit himself to mention this casually."
His intense interest in the human condition was undiminished by this situation, only the focus changed. He became to himself now, a fascinating subject for study, a phenomenon with humorous aspects. He had a new notebook to fill too—one with dosages, tests and reactions. But to his friends he presented his familiar visage.

I'll answer once and for all your eager and repeated inquiries about the hair surrounding my balls: it is soft and springy like certain mosses on warm slopes, and has the faint woody fragrance of sawdust in the sun. Now for Christ sake let's forget it.

Mrs. Williamson the lady who sleeps in the bunk just above me hollered down a minute ago and asked if I'd shit my pants. I checked and I have. So will close.

Affectionately,

Paul

Mary Fran shows the slow erosion and decay of time. They age on you, Bill. And a vinegary disposition develops. Just yesterday I said, "Sweetheart, you get homelier every minute." She said, "Go fuck yourself. You told me when we got married you had a big prick and just lookit."

I talked to Hartzell on the telephone.
I talked to Hartzell on the telephone. I guess I said that.

I visited my doctor last week. He jiggled my balls and stuck his finger up my ass. His bill will be along shortly.

R. T. McClaughery is looking for a young beautiful and passionate woman who is interested in enjoying sex at the conversation level.

Here is a slogan for Clairol, the woman's hair dye:
"Buy an extra batch and have a snatch to match."

Parke has a girl. She is a Jewish lady with a large bust. Her father is wealthy. I hope to work things out so that he puts me and all my friends in the pants business. I want to be in charge of 42 stouts. Yesterday I sought to ingratiate myself by being circumsized. I did it myself and I'm afraid I did a blotchy job.

Yes, Mrs. Thorpe, shitting your hat is a symptom of serious cranial pressure.

My wife is with child, but I am with the Indian Motorcycle people.

These years were warmed by occasional evidence that his work had not been forgotten in distinguished places, by a mention in a *New Yorker* piece on radio serials, by James Thurber, and this article in *Colliers* by John O'Hara. (excerpted):

"I offer to some Broadway producer an idea for a musical play that I would like to see. We revive those wonderfully indigenous radio characters, Vic n' Sade and their family and friends, and get Meredith Wilson to write the music. Some of those Vic n' Sade sketches were as good as Mark Twain for small town humor and a picture of life in the Midwest . . .

"And don't think there wouldn't be a message in it. There's a message in Tarkington's Penrod stories and in Sherwood Anderson's Winesburg, Ohio. The message—which will be news to a lot of people—is: That's how it was."

On November 17, 1960 Paul suffered a heart attack. Two weeks later I received a letter from him, in large scrawling handwriting:

"Old Pal:

I am propped up in bed and can scribble. The doctor says I am making satisfactory progress. However, all heart cases have to be treated as critical cases and I may have to stay on my back for some weeks to come. For a solid week I wore an oxygen con-traption and felt high like I was of martinis.

I will, of course, stand the expense of Seemah's new baby. It must be brought up in the Swedish Lutheran faith or I refuse to be responsible.

I am in a double room and this morning at four they brought in a guy who promptly died before my eyes. He had a heart attack died before my eyes. He had a heart attack but good. There was considerable traffic in and out of the room and everybody who left tiptoed solemnly and respectfully out, closing the door and extinguishing the light, leaving me in the dark with my quiet companion."

Paul suffered a second attack on December 19, 1962. He wrote from the hospital.

Well, at any rate the medical people didn't find any hemorrhoids. However, they did find traces of ring worm.

Affectionately
Paul

He also enclosed a hospital dinner menu, on the back of which there was a handwritten note:

"Dear Patient Rhymer:

We are asking you to discontinue your habit of using the hot buttered pocket-book rolls as a device for self-abuse.

The Hospital Management"

Feb. 7, 1964 (after 2nd attack)

I came home from the hospital a week ago. My friend Jack Dunn and a big young bruiser from the Chicago Historical Society carried me up the stairs on a kitchen chair. I should have reflected that Dunn is 55 years old, overweight and an ulcer sufferer. He certainly panted and wheezed going up those fucking steps. Wouldn't it have been funny if he'd fallen over dead?

March 4, 1963

I am to be best man at the wedding of Jack Dunn who is 55. The bride is 30. She loves the faint half flush that dies along his throat.

A third attack occurred on August 28, 1963. He wrote to his friend Stanley Meyer:

"Well, I had a pulmonary oedema. You'll recall from your expensive medical education at Marquette that the condition involves a flooding of the lungs with fluid and a poor half-wit dam near drowns.

I've now had three coronary occlusions and this makes a guy somewhat thoughtful. Of course, on the cheery side I can't help reflecting that if I've survived three why can't I survive 127? It's Blue Cross' ass, not mine."

And in a letter to me:

> "Mary Fran heard a group of my doctors discussing my case out in the hall. One was saying gravely: 'It's between Paul and his Maker now.'
>
> "Actually I feel fine and expect to be discharged from the hospital this coming Saturday. I guess I told you I had a pulmonary oedema. That's where a half-wit's lungs fill up with fluid and he dam near drowns. I was rushed here in an ambulance, gasping and moaning. I tried to get up on my elbow to look out the window but the guy sitting on my chest shoved me back, remarking, 'Take it easy, daddeo.' That ambulance trip cost me $28.00. But we made plenty noise and folks got out of the way.
>
> "I believe the opinion in the hospital is that this last attack damaged my wits. Guys in white jackets hold up a forefinger and say: 'What is this?'
>
> "'It's Mrs. John J. Kennedy's twat,' I holler.
>
> "'That's right,' they rejoin. And then they take out their cock and jack off in their hat."

In another letter from the hospital at this time he wrote to his friend Don Weldon:

> My friend Jack Dunn gave me a book called "The History of Surgery." It says that in 1900 no women were examined by doctors. It was thought too indelicate. However, about 1905 a physician named Clyde Sims achieved the big breathrough. He not only undressed a woman patient and examined her private parts but he also invented a device for holding the vagina open so he could sit in his goddamn rocking chair and stare all day if he felt like it. Every physician in the world has one of these devices as regular office equipment. I believe it is called "The Clyde Sims Little Daisy Twat Spreader."

"Below is a rare picture of old Clyde examining a snatch.

"Weldon, I thought we might write a play about Clyde Sims and his career. He ended up a millionaire, of course, but I figure he must have been a pool hall bum to let his mind wander in such areas. I won't make any reference to your sister but a person grows white-lipped and trembling to think of her making an appointment with old Clyde Sims.

Affectionately

Paul"

April 22, 1964

Jack Dunn will die soon. He has cancer of the lung and of the brain. It all came galloping. A month ago Jack was fine. He's still fine, full of pep. He doesn't know the condition he's in but I expect he must be doing some smart guessing. Because of his enormous vitality he's been on top of the situation. I get bulletins on the sly from his wife. It's disconcerting to have her telephone and tell me something horrible has developed and then have Jack call and invite me to lunch in Forest Park. Yesterday was the first time I saw Jack in actual pain. My friend Merlin Bowen and I paid him a call. He asked his wife for cigarette, took a drag, had a coughing fit and went into a spasm of agony. I'm told they hope the brain cancer moves rapidly and cuts off the anguish. Isn't this awful? I haven't written to anybody about it. Later on in the day I'll probably talk to Jack on the horn and he'll be full of jolly jokes and ambitious plans. He'd be astonished if he could read this letter. I am, kind of, myself.

Another attack came on December 25, 1963. He wrote to Stanley Meyer:

"My physician doesn't seem alarmed about recurrences of oedema. He simply tells me to order the ambulance for every morning at five o'clock; if the driver sees that the curtain is pulled down he can go on about his business. If the curtain is in a normal position he is supposed to stop past and pick up the body."

There was yet another attack on October 20, 1964. And on October 27 came the telegram that made me put my face in my hands and weep.

> "Paul died peacefully last night. Funeral Graceland Chapel Thursday 2:30. From Carrolla 25 East Erie. Love. Mary Francis Rhymer."

Early in 1964 I had to go to Chicago on business involving the sale of my father's saloon in Forest Park. For several days I stayed with Paul at Phil Schmidt's restaurant, I was able to say to Paul something I'd wanted to tell him for many, many years.

"You're my ace in the hole," I said. "When things are not going well, and people don't seem to like me much, I can always make myself feel better by thinking that I must be worth something because I'm your friend."

Paul just nodded.

When I left to drive back to the airport in my rented Ford Coupe, I looked up in the rear-view mirror and saw him standing on the street corner, keeping me in sight as long as he could, a white-haired, dignified man in a dark topcoat and dark felt hat and I had a strong, almost overwhelming feeling that his was the last time I'd see him.

```
547P PST OCT 27 64 LA397 OB615 MB564
M CA737 RX PD CHICAGO ILL 27 653P CST
MR AND MRS WILLIAM IDELSON
   710 BROOKTREE RD PACIFIC PALISADES CALIF
PAUL DIED PEACEFULLY LAST NIGHT. FUNERAL GRACELAND CHAPEL THURSDAY
230. FROM CARROLLS 25 EAST ERIE. LOVE
   MARY FRANCES RHYMER
KPOLM
```

www.ingramcontent.com/pod-product-compliance
Lightning Source LLC
Chambersburg PA
CBHW050336230426
43663CB00010B/1882